T0115258

Parenthood Unplanned

A SURVIVAL GUIDE FOR THE UNEXPECTED

SARAH DUNFORD

Post Hill
PRESS

A POST HILL PRESS BOOK
ISBN: 978-1-64293-487-8
ISBN (eBook): 978-1-64293-488-5

Parenthood Unplanned:
A Survival Guide for the Unexpected
© 2020 by Sarah Dunford
All Rights Reserved

Author photo by Megan and Dallas Photography

Post Hill Press
New York • Nashville
posthillpress.com

Published in the United States of America

Dad, the soul by whom I measure all men—

*I am fully aware of the depth of God's love for me
because of your example. Thanks, Dad.*

*Barbara—for loving Miranda as your own and showing
me what a blended family should look like.*

*Mom—For being so comfortable in your own skin,
you weren't afraid to be the black sheep.*

We miss you every day.

TABLE OF CONTENTS

CHAPTER 1

The Gift of You

My dad died three years ago. It was the most devastating thing I have ever experienced. He was a good man. He was a humble man. He didn't say a whole lot. He never learned to read or even write much. He never finished tenth grade because he was dyslexic. He came from a very large, poor family. When I was a child, he worked in a manufacturing plant until a chemical spill put him out of work. He would get up and hitchhike for hours to get to work if our car wasn't running for some reason. I know this because during my elementary school years, he would wake me to lock the door behind him when he left for work while my mom and siblings were still sleeping. I was the easiest one to wake and the easiest one to fall right back to sleep! Despite all the troubles and shortcomings he had in his life, he looked at me and saw potential. He didn't have much in life, but he did some awesome things in his own way. The first was that he set the foundation for my value. It was a gift and I would like to share it with you. He let me know I was something special. He made me feel like I could do anything and be anything I wanted.

One example of how he instilled that belief happened in 1984. I was eight years old, sitting on a couch, watching the Olympics. My favorite competitors were the figure skaters. In my opinion, they were spectacular, graceful, and elegant. They reminded me of ballerinas, except on ice. I loved them. My dad walked in and sat down beside me, and after watching for a bit, we started chatting about what they were doing and how hard it must be. He leaned over and said, "Who knows, someday we may be watching you up there." No, I did not go to the Olympics, but I never needed to—it was enough to believe I could have if I had wanted to.

I want to give you the gift that my father gave me. I want you to know that regardless of your circumstances, you are capable of being and doing anything. Anything. If you should choose to, you have the ability to rise above handicaps, shortcomings, and statistics that will want to put you in a box and tell you that you cannot change the path you are on or forge a new path, if you choose to do so. But you are strong! You are one good decision from something beautiful. You are one good decision from that door opening, that path revealing itself, or from that cloud that seems to hang over your head completely dissipating.

There was a point in my life when I felt I had made a complete mess of everything: finances, relationships, and everything else. I ended up in my pastor's office, sitting on his couch, telling him all my mistakes and failures. And he, being the eternal optimist that he is, gave me this advice:

"Sarah, you have made some mistakes and bad decisions, but here's the thing. Life is like a garden.

Your garden is a result of what you have planted. The bad decisions you have made have choked out the good decisions. Whatever you plant will grow. Don't worry about trying to fix it all today. When you wake up tomorrow, start planting good seeds. Make one good decision tomorrow. Then the next day, do the same thing. Eventually, your garden will be beautiful again and all the good decisions will choke out all the bad ones."

This was some of the greatest advice I ever received. It helped me understand a few things.

1. I don't have to fix it all at once.

2. One good decision every day will eventually add up.

3. Even if life is a mess now, good things are on their way—so be patient.

If your life, at this moment, is less than ideal, with a long trail of disappointments and failures, take heart! You are at the perfect place for God to show up and do great things on your behalf. Invite Him into your mess. He is not afraid of your mistakes. He is big enough. He is mighty enough. He is all that you need. Do what you can, and when you have done all that you can do, get out of His way!

We are going to do an exercise together. We are going to make an outline of who you are because you are probably hearing that nagging voice in your head telling you all the things you aren't. You may be pregnant unexpectedly, finding yourself single with two mouths to feed, and overwhelmed with the idea of holding it all together. Or you may be recently remarried and at the end of a week of battles in your house that you were not expecting. That is when the voice starts dripping like a leaky faucet that is getting on the last nerve you have. The time to sit down and take stock of who you are is now. Jessica Andrews sings a song titled, "Who I Am." Her song is a list that does this exact thing. The lyrics are powerful, and I encourage you to give the song a listen when you're trying to come up with your own list.

Humor me for a moment. Get a piece of paper and try to do an outline for yourself! The goal is to get a firm understanding of who you are. It looks just like the song. Here is mine:

» I am a daughter of the King of all Kings.

» I am Clyde and Charlene's daughter.

» I am the baby girl.

» I am a West Virginia Mountaineer till I die!

» I am a teacher.

» I am a fighter.

» I am creative.

» I am a writer.

» I am a mom.

» I am a little sister.

» I am a big sister.

» I am fearless.

» I make people laugh.

» I may make people cry.

» I am quick-witted.

» I am loyal. Like mafia-style loyal.

The most important part of your parenting journey begins with your foundation. You need a clear understanding of your identity and your value! I believe that for you to make the best decision possible, you must first know who *you* are and *your value*. You may not realize the extent of your uniqueness. You are a treasure. You are precious. Your value is not predicated upon what you do or how you make others feel. You are these things because your value is intrinsic—simply because you are.

At the end of the day, you have a story. Your story should not be written by anyone but you. Your story will be unlike anyone else's. It will look different than anyone else's. It will sound different than anyone else. It will read different than anyone else's story. It is supposed to be that way!

God's gift to the world is you, and what you do with that life is your gift to Him. The world needs what you have. Your hands, your heart, your laugh…they are needed by someone, somewhere, at some time. Even with all the flaws and mistakes, you are still the apple of God's eye. When He looks you in the eyes, He sees a reflection of his beautiful creation. He loves you very much and wants only great things for you! Canadian psychologist Jordan Peterson said it best when he said, "You fill a hole in the world that is exactly your shape."

I'm not trying to beat a dead horse, but you need to hear what I am telling you! You reflect God's creation. Read that last sentence again. Now again. You have greatness inside of you. You are stronger than you know. Sure, you may not be ruling a country or traveling the globe on some medical mission team. Your day may begin and end with a pile of laundry on the couch and a baby at your feet. I am sure the mother of every world-changer did the exact same things. You never know—you could be raising the next president, the next doctor to change the world with his or her medical breakthrough, the next really decent neighbor or the next helping hand to someone in need. (Side note: if your child never does any of these things, it doesn't matter because their value is very much like your own: inherent, simply because they are.) Every mother simply chooses to have faith. She chooses faith the moment she gives birth. She chooses faith the moment she chooses adoption for her child. She chooses faith the moment she starts the arduous journey of raising a child that will change her life forever, in the hope that all she wants for them comes to pass and that she makes all the right choices along the way. These are the hallmarks of strength. I tip my hat to you, ladies!

I say all of this to acknowledge that the struggle is real, but so is the triumph. I know that despite all that life can throw at you, life is still *beautiful.* I know I wouldn't trade the twenty-six years of looking into my daughter's eyes for anything on this planet. (Even if some of those years weren't pleasant.) I wouldn't trade the faith-building miracles I have seen along this road called young motherhood or single motherhood for anything. Those miracles got me thinking I could finish school. I thought, *surely if God got me through that, He can get me through school.* He did! I sat in class after class repeating, "Greater is He that is in me!" It was during those years that I watched as God put the perfect people in my life at the perfect time to help my daughter avoid becoming a statistic, and it happened all the time.

Just a few examples of this:

We had a couple that owned a convenience store in my church, and unprovoked and without cause, they would show up with a bag of candy from their store for my daughter. Every Sunday, Jay would bring her a bag and tell her to put it away until she got home. In fourth grade, my daughter had a teacher—a great male example when she needed one. On the last day of school, he came to our home and taped a poster he'd had on his wall for his entire teaching career, with a note on the back from top to bottom telling her how much he believed in her. (Truth be told, she harassed him the entire year for it.) One time, when she was in third grade, I received a large box in the mail from one of my childhood friends. Kristi, unprovoked, got together with some others and sent a huge box of school supplies. My other childhood friend, Marilyn, spent countless hours loving on my daughter, taking her on hiking trips, and much more. To this day I see certain traits in my daughter that came from people who invested in her. God was always on time, every time.

One final Dad story as we wrap things up. Not too long before my father passed away, I was at his house and he was having a very rough day. My dad, a man of very few words, decided to let me know he had something to tell me. He said, "Sarah, if things don't end well with me…well…you know that I have *loved* you, right?" Such a simple sentence; nothing to fall apart over. Except that it was the way he said it that stopped me in my tracks. It was as if he stopped the world and made everything pause just long enough to tell his baby girl, he loved her. We just looked at each other, frozen for a second. It was like he wanted to say, "Everything that I am or have ever been *has loved,* and will love, everything that you are or will become—forever." I cried. He got tears in his eyes and I leaned in and hugged him. I explained to him that I was aware of how big God's love was for me because of his example of love. Dad passed away three weeks later. It was one of his final gifts to me. He needed to make sure before he left this life that I knew I was loved.

No matter who your father is or is not, is of no consequence because we all have a father that feels this way about us. God loves you with a deep, relentless, faithful love. All that He is loves all that you are and ever hope to be. Your guilt does not sway him. Your mistakes, mishaps, flaws, sin, and blunders, these do not sway Him or His love for you. All of you.

CHAPTER 2

Taming Emotions

If a pregnant girl can be called anything, it would be emotional. Your body is, after all, making a human being. You've earned a pass on crying, laughing, crying again, and laughing once more for good measure—all in one conversation. This can happen in ideal situations. If you are in a less than ideal situation those emotions are not just there, they are *there* and they are magnified.

In this chapter, we are going to address some of the emotions and feelings that come to anyone in the middle of an unexpected pregnancy. Often, the words trying to take root in your mind are self-defeating lies that grow bigger and bigger.

When my daughter was young, she would watch a cartoon over and over again about a character that lies. The lie, which was a small little thing, grew every time the character lied to cover up the first lie until it became so large it was wrecking his town. There came a point when the character finally came clean by telling the truth. Every time he told the truth about all the lies, the monster shrunk.

Left unchecked, the lies you hear in your head become like the lie in that cartoon, wrecking the places of your mind until you are defeated before you have even begun to fight. All you really need to do is speak the truth to the lie when you hear it whispered or shouted in your ear. You will be amazed at how fast that huge, fearful thing shrinks down to size in the light of truth.

We are going to answer these emotions and lies with truth until we drown them out and can no longer hear them!

We are going to start with the emotions that will back you into a corner, make you feel like you have no way out and before you know it, the lies will have you making decisions you do not want to make.

The Lie: Fear is Here to Stay.

Being fearful is defined as feeling afraid: showing fear or anxiety. Being terrified is defined as feeling extremely fearful.

The Truth

We can allow fear to overcome us in any difficult situation when we are confronted with the unknown. It could be marriage. It could be an illness. It could be taking a test. It could be death. Fear that is paralyzing is a phobia. Your scary unknown, if you are reading this book, is probably an unexpected pregnancy. Regardless if your situation is great or not so great, we all have fear with a pregnancy. More importantly, we need to recognize that many times, it's not just the pregnancy that is the issue; rather, it is what will be said, the reaction of others, or the fear that we have let someone down. There are two great ways to combat fear. First, view every situation through a long-term lens. How will this look in ten years? How will this look in twenty years? If you don't know how this will look, find someone in a similar situation and ask them how it ended up looking for them with the passage of time. Second, as a Christian, I always seek God and His Word for my answers. My greatest battles were won not because I was a spiritual guru or because I had it all together and ran straight to His Word. It was usually my last option. I tried everything else. In my desperation, I cried out to God and he heard my prayer. It was never in the way I thought it would be, but He does *hear* and He does answer. He is faithful and so is His Word.

Scripture Reference

John 14:27
"Peace I leave with you; my peace I give you. I do not give to you as the world gives. Do not let your hearts be troubled and do not be afraid."

The Lie: You Are Not Strong Enough to Do This.

Weakness is defined as the inability to do or achieve (something), or, alternatively, the inability to behave rationally or manage one's affairs; incompetence.

The Truth

Our heroes, no matter which ones we think of, are triumphant. They struggle and they fight, but finally, they are victorious, and that is what makes them our heroes. As a history major in college, I was always intrigued by the lives of the people that accomplished great things more than the things they accomplished. My grades weren't fantastic because I was always side-tracked with the backstory. I wanted to hear about the struggle and the triumph. When I read stories of people who struggle and prevail, I am, along with most people, impressed and inspired. Helen Keller, Corrie Ten Boom, Harriet Tubman, and Abraham Lincoln are just a handful of examples. Although they may never make the front-page news, everyday people living everyday lives are doing the heroic. A single mom making it through school to graduate with a baby on her hip. A single mom watching her daughter graduate from college after years of struggle. Eleanor Roosevelt said it best: "A woman is like a tea bag—you can't tell how strong she is until you put her in hot water."

Scripture References

Psalm 46:1–3

"God is our refuge and strength, an ever-present help in trouble. Therefore, we will not fear, though the earth give way and the mountains fall into the heart of the sea, though its waters roar and foam and the mountains quake with their surging."

Philippians 4:13

"I can do all things through Christ which strengthens me."

The Lie: You are Guilty and Ought to Be Ashamed.

Guilt is defined as the fact of having committed a specified or implied offense or crime. *Shame* is defined as a painful feeling of humiliation or distress caused by the consciousness of wrong or foolish behavior.

The Truth

These two, guilt and shame, are the ones that make you wish you could cover your face and refuse to see your accusers forever. Although others may judge you, your biggest accuser is usually the one looking back at you in the mirror. Cut her some slack; we are all full of things in our lives that make us want to run and hide if we are being honest. Although you do have responsibility, you are innocent in God's eyes when you confess to Him. Although you cannot change what has been done, you can speak life and abundance to your future. If you are a believer, fall back on His Word.

Have radical faith. See what others do not for your life. We can choose to see everything that is wrong—all the dark, dreadful, painful things—or we can simply choose to see something else. We can choose to see the good and speak the good over us, our children, our lives, our futures. We can be innocent of making more wrong choices. We can be innocent of accepting that voice we hear in our heads. We can live humbly and without shame in a life dependent upon Christ and His Word. We can grow wiser through our experience and help the next girl we see in the same situation we were once in.

Scripture Reference

Psalm 103:8–12

"The Lord is merciful and gracious; slow to anger and abounding in steadfast love. He will not always chide, nor will He keep His anger forever. He does not deal with us according to our sins, nor repay us according to our iniquities. For as high as the heavens are above the earth, so great is His steadfast love toward those who fear Him; as far as the east is from the west, so far does He remove our transgressions from us."

Ezekiel Chapter 37

The Lie: You Are Abandoned and Alone.

Abandoned is defined as having been deserted or cast off. Being alone is defined as having no one else present, or on one's own.

The Truth

You may feel very much alone. It may be true that you may not have a support system in place *at this time*. We are taught in the Christian faith that we are never alone. That Jesus is by our sides. The longer I live, the more depth I see in this scripture. It is not simply black letters typed against white paper. It is a vibrant verse that resembles a kaleidoscope held up against the light of a brilliant sky and looked through. The color and shape of it changes as it turns, bringing happiness to the viewer. You are never alone.

You are right in the palm of His hand. You are hidden in the shadow of His wings. You are in the perfect place for miracles. I heard someone say once that everyone loves a miracle but no one wants to be put in a place where they need one. Need a miracle? Can't see the ones happening in your life right now? Keep looking. He is working on your behalf.

Scripture References

Romans 8:38–39

"For I am persuaded, that neither death, nor life, nor angels, nor principalities, nor powers, nor things present, nor things to come, Nor height, nor depth, nor any other creature, shall be able to separate us from the love of God, which is in Christ Jesus our Lord."

Deuteronomy 31:6

"Be strong and of a good courage, fear not, nor be afraid of them: for the Lord thy God, he it is that doth go with thee; he will not fail thee, nor forsake thee."

The Lie: You Deserve to Be Humiliated.

To be *humiliated* is defined as to be made to feel ashamed and foolish through an injury to one's dignity and self-respect, especially in public. Humiliation can sometimes come through some sort of betrayal.

The Truth

There is nothing quite like the emotions that come from being humiliated or betrayed. Nothing can build an impenetrable wall on one's life like this ugly monster. It creates suspicion and distrust in a person's life like nothing else. I know. In my life, it helped me build walls so tall that they made the Empire State Building look like child's play. Literally, the only thing getting in was Almighty God himself, and I am pretty sure during his rescue attempt I heard Him beating His head against those walls I had built. Think Fort Knox or Alcatraz.

If you are facing humiliation or betrayal from those closest to you, take heart. You are not alone, and you're in good company in this club. Even Christ was betrayed. You can choose to see nothing but the betrayal, or you can choose to look around it. Look forward to your future. Sit down and write a list of your biggest goals. Write Plan A on how to reach those goals. Don't forget to have Plans B, C, and D lined up, because you probably will need them as well. But do not allow dream thieves to steal your life; do not let their betrayal crush your spirit. As hard as it is to do this, leave those dreams and that spirit in God's hands. Here's why. In the case of an unexpected pregnancy—after the surprise and shock have worn off and a beautiful little cherub shows up giggling and toddling around the house—hard hearts begin to melt. What seemed like an impossibility starts holding your hand and saying your name. All that angst will melt away. Here's a key you need to remember. If by chance, the people in your life are determined to stay away or will not allow a crack in their resolve, they are the ones that will be losing in the long term. They will be robbed of the joy, love, and excitement of every milestone they miss. I know this may not help heal your heart in the present, but your heart *will* heal. You *will* recover. You *will* be OK. There is nothing special about me. I am not extraordinary in any way. If I can make it, I promise you, you *can* make it. I do not doubt what I am telling you for a second. This is a season. This too shall pass.

Scripture References

Micah 7:8

"Rejoice not over me, O my enemy; when I fall, I shall rise; when I sit in darkness, the Lord will be a light to me."

Mark 11:25

"And when ye stand praying, forgive, if ye have ought against any: that your Father also which is in heaven may forgive you your trespasses."

The Lie: God Doesn't Care About What's Going on in Your Life.

There are several definitions for the word *care* depending on how it is used, but in this case, we will use *painstaking or watchful attention.*

The Truth

He is in the smallest details in all our lives. He painstakingly looks over us even if we push Him away or run in another direction. It may seem like God is way far away from you and that He doesn't care about where you are or what is happening because your world is imploding, but His Word tells us differently. Often times, we choose not to see God working to salvage the mess we have made. We should be expecting greatness from God because He is great and does great things!

When I was a newlywed, my husband and I were trying to make good decisions. We saved some money for a down payment on our first home. We wanted to make the right choices, so we bought our first home, a cute little Victorian townhouse on the south side of Richmond, Virginia. We were so happy and so thankful to be buying our own place. The problem was, while I didn't want to be ungrateful, it had hideous wallpaper straight from the 1980s on the walls. It was navy blue with these white curved lines that looked like toenail clippings scattered across it. I was eight months pregnant and I knew it would be months before I would have the energy to tackle taking it down. My legs were swollen, we were about to spend days moving, and I was exhausted just thinking about it. I hate removing wallpaper. I remember standing with my face pressed up against the sliding glass doors on the patio and looking in the living room, a little disappointed in that hideous paper. I prayed a prayer that day that was more like a daughter asking a dad for something: "Lord, I am so thankful for my new home, but it would be really great if you could do something about that wallpaper, It's awful." That was it. I chuckled, got in my car, and went home to wait for closing day.

About two weeks later, I got a call; it was the realtor asking me if I could meet some workers at the townhouse to pick out my paint and new carpet because there had been an issue with the townhouse: a water leak in the living room. So, I did what any curious person would do, and I drove over and found myself looking through those glass doors again. I couldn't believe my eyes. The wallpaper that I hated was in perfect piles on the floor along the wall where the water leak ran down. The water had caused all that old wallpaper to slide right down the walls. I was in utter disbelief. He heard my prayer and removed the paper for me and decided to throw in new paint and carpet as well because He and I both knew I didn't have the money to get new paint and carpet. Start believing that God hears you, cares for you, and that He answers prayers.

Scripture References

Philippians 4:6

"Be anxious for nothing, but in everything by prayer and supplication with thanksgiving let your requests be made known to God."

1 Samuel 1:20

"Wherefore it came to pass, when the time was come about after Hannah had conceived, that she bare a son, and called his name Samuel, *saying*, Because I have asked him of the LORD."

Hebrews 4:16

"Let us therefore come boldly unto the throne of grace, that we may obtain mercy, and find grace to help in time of need."

CHAPTER 3

Fierce and Feminine

In an attempt to point out a woman's uniqueness and her value in and of itself, my research sent me down a rabbit hole of definition-hunting. I want to share some definitions of words we use all the time. First, we will start with the title of this chapter.

> **Fierce:** (of a feeling, emotion, or action): showing a heartfelt and powerful intensity.

> **Feminine:** having qualities or appearance traditionally associated with women, especially delicacy and prettiness.

These are the foundational words I use when building up all things female, and in my mind, what should be the poster children for the modern feminist movement. The movement couldn't be anti-man because the very definition of it requires something for women to be equal to. That, of course, would be men.

> **Feminism:** the advocacy of women's rights on the basis of the *equality of the sexes*.

> **Equality:** the state of being equal, especially in *status, rights, and opportunities*.

Feminism is not a bad thing, in its original definition and intent, but if I could change this definition, it would simply read: the advocacy of a women's rights. The way the definition reads sets us up for a battle in comparison. I want my rights because they are mine, not because they were a man's first. The fight used to be for equal rights under the law, laws that needed to be established, such as laws prohibiting men from beating women. Men can't take women's children without cause. Men can't leave women destitute after they spend their career years raising and taking care of the children at home. Women can pursue careers as long as their strength and brains can get them the job. Women can hold property. Women can serve on the Supreme Court. Women have the right to vote.

Unfortunately, what we currently see played out time and again is that it has turned into a game of preference and/or power. I have literally seen signs that say, "The future is female." It looks like the end goal for the modern feminist movement is for the world to be monochromatic. It's as if we all should have been born male. No that can't be right; it's feminism. As if we all should have been born female. That's the ticket.

It would be comical, if it weren't so sad, that the modern feminist movement screams for diversity and acceptance until a man walks in the room. Then the movement is more than willing to strip away the rights of the individual simply because he was born with the wrong parts. Wait, wasn't that what they were fighting against?

The simple truth is this. Our strengths are not theirs. Yes, we should be equal under the law. Yes, we should have the same rights as men. Yes, we should have the same opportunities as them. However, they were never meant to be what we are and we were never meant to be what they are. Women's accomplishments must stop being measured by what a man has done first. We cannot say we are great in our own right if what we are great at is only great because we do what a man did first. Let me clarify for you with one tiny example. A young mom tackles the arduous tasks of breastfeeding. This is her accomplishment alone. Something her husband can never do and something her husband certainly hasn't done first. We are the only human beings capable of doing that, as well as carrying a baby or giving birth. It is unique to us. It is beautiful. This is a small example, but look on a larger scale and find something around you that a woman has done in her own right and not because a man did it first. Ladies, there is more to us than "being the first woman to" as compared with a man.

This brutal game of comparison has deconstructed social safety nets such as marriage, proposals, and abstinence, and actually encourages behaviors that make the woman's life much harder, such as single motherhood, poverty, crime, and so forth. The list goes on and on. It completely removes the social responsibility from the men and allows women to be taken advantage of under the guise of helping the women out. A man doesn't have to support a woman or be held accountable for his actions, regardless of what choice the woman makes. I am amazed at girls who can't stand irresponsible men, and yet give them the opportunity to be irresponsible. The woman will be the one affected, whether physically, emotionally, or both. It is not her body, her choice; it never was. It is a woman being trapped and being *forced* to make a decision. Meanwhile, the irresponsible man conveniently leans back and says, "Her body, her choice." After all, it's not his body, his choice. It is a catchy slogan, though. Do you see that this idea has actually made things worse, not better, for the *woman*?

Real talk for a minute: she will be put on a table an abortion will be performed. She will give birth and raise that child alone. She will make a parenting plan for her child unless they both get mature real fast and decide to start a family. She will forever carry around the weight of "her choice." Her body will be forever changed either way, and all the social safety nets built to protect her are being dismantled one by one with overly simplified slogans that take a very complex matter and make it seem inconsequential. It is time to rebuild those social safety nets burning faster than a wildfire in August. The point, ladies, to this entire chapter is that not only should you not be comparing and measuring yourself and your life by other women's lives, but you shouldn't be doing that with men's lives either. The *only* competition you have is *you* in five years!

Over the next few chapters, we are going look at some real-life experiences that some pretty amazing women were willing to share with me. Some of them are hard stories to tell, and some of them will be hard to read. But I believe that the truth sets us free. As you read, I want you to know they are true stories, told to me by real flesh-and-blood women who are living out their lives. When you are faced with an unplanned pregnancy, you have choices you will have to make. The wisest thing anyone can do is learn lessons and make better choices from someone else's story.

We are going to look at:

1. Women who chose to parent.

2. Women who chose abortion and what that looks like years later.

3. Adoption stories from both the adopting mother and the girl or woman choosing adoption for her baby.

All three scenarios are being played out around you and on a daily basis. They are worth pausing to examine before you choose the road you will travel down.

CHAPTER 4

Parenting: Our Stories

Deanna • Sarah • Bella*

*Names changed to protect privacy

Deanna

I was in eleventh grade and seventeen years old when my friend called me, crying. She was bawling and afraid. It was a one-night stand and she had discovered she was pregnant. She said, "This cannot get out and I need you to go with me to my appointment." We both knew that if it got out, she would be labeled a slut and a piece of trash—let alone the wrath of her family that she'd have to endure. We went to her appointment, and while I parked the car and went to the waiting room, my friend viewed a video about what was about to happen—and she came out shaking and crying but told me she had to do this. She went in for the procedure and came out crying, pale, and shaking. She was sick and she didn't want to talk about it. We never talked about it again. It was a dirty little secret we had to keep. My heart broke for her.

Later, the summer after high school graduation, I received yet another call from a crying friend. She had missed her period, and her boyfriend took her to get a pregnancy test. It was positive. She was an only child and a daddy's girl. She was sure her father would never forgive her. She didn't work so she had no way to support herself, and she wasn't sure that her boyfriend was faithful. When she told him she was pregnant, he wasn't interested in taking responsibility and couldn't be bothered to take her to the closest abortion facility. So, she broke up with him, and I drove her down to the facility. Once again, my friend viewed the video of the procedure she was about to have done. She came back into the waiting room very shaken up and pale. They called her back and when she returned, she was shaking and crying. The first thing she said to me after the procedure was that she was going to be sick. She and I went to the bathroom, where she threw up. I knew I could never have an abortion, but I was really trying to help my friends. That night, my friend begged me to spend the night with her so her family would leave her alone. She needed someone to talk with. She talked about how bad it hurt both emotionally and physically. She talked a lot about how everything made her feel.

When I saw the effect that abortion had on my friends, it left me brokenhearted. It felt like I was losing someone and it only solidified how I could never make that choice. I have thought of them over the years. We lost touch for a long time and I wondered if it haunted them. I had my own battles in life. I was wild. I spent time going to parties and finding ways to get into trouble. It wasn't too long after that that I found myself in the same pregnancy situation my friends had faced. I was at a party and I met a guy. I was fighting at home with my dad and mom until it got so bad that one day, I was telling my boyfriend about it and he told me he would get an apartment and we could move in together. The fighting continued at home, even after I moved out until eventually, my mom moved in with us.

One particular night after having too much to drink, I woke up not remembering what happened the night before. I didn't have any clothes on, so something definitely happened. My boyfriend knew though. He told me that he didn't use protection and that he had given me a baby. I was furious and started screaming at him. We had a huge fight that day. I felt so disrespected that he would make that decision without my agreement. It wasn't too long after that I started having symptoms, and by the time I missed my period, I knew I was pregnant.

After calling a friend to get advice, I took a test and it came back positive. The first person I told was my mother. My mother's response was to tell me, "You know what you are going to have to do." She told me all the ramifications of this pregnancy. She told me that my father would never speak to me again and that the family would judge me and have a lot to say. The father of the baby and his family were from a foreign country that would reject our marriage and disown any children from the union. I heard him and his mother arguing in Arabic and raising their voices with one another. Both sides of our family were angry over it. My boyfriend decided we should get married to try to make things right and make our families happy. I was about three months along when we went down to the justice of the peace and had a quick ceremony.

My father was very angry and point-blank asked if I was getting married because I was pregnant. He wanted to know what I was going to do about what the family was going to say until finally I had enough and I told him I didn't see my family enough for their opinion to matter. Once a year at a family reunion was not enough to make me get rid of this pregnancy. On the back porch amongst the roses that day, amongst the flowers that he loved and tended, my father and I made peace.

Three months later, my husband decided that he wanted me to meet his family, so we traveled to Kuwait to meet them. He would tell stories about how beautiful his home was and how I was going to love it. We flew in at night and all we could see were the wells that had been set on fire burning. He sat in the seat next to me looking out, agonizing over what was happening to his home. The next morning in the light of day, you could see the devastation from bombings and war. Soldiers were everywhere. You couldn't go on the beach because landmines had been buried out there. Things started changing very fast. The family wanted me to change the clothes I was wearing. They wanted my jeans and my makeup gone. I was forced to wear a hijab to go outside. I was pregnant and craving home. I faced intense scrutiny from his family as they tried to convince me that my belief system was all wrong. They had a Quran and would kind of mock me and the Jesus I believed in. I wasn't a scholar and I didn't know the Bible. All I knew was that I loved Jesus and that He was with me and that He had always been with me. They would eventually drop the subject.

I felt like a prisoner. I had to walk behind my husband and wear a hijab when we went out. He told me people would give me a hard time if they found out I was American. I craved chocolate and wanted familiar surroundings.

I went to get away and take a bath one evening. I was about six months along and as I was getting out of the tub I slipped and fell. I got on their intercom system and yelled that I needed help. My mother-in-law told us something would be wrong with the baby because of the fall. It was awful. I was taken to the hospital but my husband couldn't go with me. They didn't allow men back where the women were, so I went with my husband's sister-in-law, and no one spoke English. I don't remember a lot about the hospital visit but I do remember it was just very different.

At this point, my mother and the U.S. Embassy that she had contacted were calling on a regular basis to make sure I was OK and that I wasn't being held against my will or being abused. Before our wedding, I had discovered when we were getting our marriage license that my soon-to-be husband had lied about his age. I wasn't afraid for my life because I was pretty sure if things got physical, I could take him, even at six months pregnant. The problem was that I was getting to the point in my pregnancy where the doctors wouldn't let me fly. My mom was very fearful that if I had my baby over there that I would never get to bring her home to the States. I knew she was right. She had to increase her credit limit on her credit card to get me home, but she booked me a flight.

I cannot begin to describe to you the relief I felt getting off the airplane when we landed at Dulles International Airport back in Northern Virginia. The moment I saw them, I ran into my mom and dad's arms and cried. To be back in America was amazing. My husband later got back to the States in time for the baby's birth. I had picked out the name Julianna Nicole but the moment she was born, he picked out the name Saurah. He told me she would be picked on in Kuwait with a name like Julianna. He told me that they do not do middle names over there, so I could give her whatever middle name I wanted. On November 27, Saurah Noelle was born. My husband's visa had expired and he had to leave. I told him I wanted to be home for Christmas. But I promised to make it to Kuwait after Christmas. I took him to the airport and he said his goodbyes to the both of us. I got in my car; as I was leaving, I pulled over on the side of the road to watch his plane take off, and I sobbed. I knew in my heart it was goodbye. I never made it back to Kuwait and he never made it back here. Eventually, our relationship disintegrated.

My baby and I lived with my mom and dad. My dad took to Saurah like a fish to water. It was love at first sight from the moment she was born. He took her everywhere. She was always with Grandma and Papaw. She was Papaw's little "Saurahlita." She was his buddy. I would watch him with her and think that all the grief and the stress when I found out I was pregnant was for nothing. She brought us so much joy! I was content with the life I had after that first marriage. It was years before I was ready to get married again.

When Saurah was about ten months old, I met the man that would become my husband. We would be together four years before I was even close to being ready to get married again. We got pregnant and when he proposed, I turned him down. He was floored. Regardless of it all, he was persistent and consistent in his love for me and my girl. By the time I was six months along, he had convinced me that he was here to stay. We got married before our son arrived. Five years later, we welcomed another baby girl in the world! It has been twenty-six years and we are going still going strong.

Over the years, I have reached out to girls that have gotten pregnant unexpectedly. I always remember where I came from and what I went through. I always make sure that I encourage them so that they know they are not alone. I make sure they have a soft place to land or shoulder to cry on.

My Story (Sarah)

I was fifteen and married when I got pregnant with my daughter. She was born two weeks to the day after my sixteenth birthday. I was poor as dirt. I had no health insurance. I went down to the local Planned Parenthood because I had no idea what they did and who they were. I got a pregnancy test performed by a nurse who asked me what I was going to do with the baby. I didn't understand the question. I thought, *What a strange question.* So, I shrugged my shoulders, trying to figure out how to answer such a stupid question and carefully answered, "Raise it. What else do you do with a baby?"

There was a long, awkward silence. It dawned on both of us that I was in a place that got rid of babies and was clueless about it. I must have appeared country as cornbread to that nurse. I can hear her now after I left. "Whelp, that one was straight off the farm." I couldn't get dressed and get out of there fast enough.

On July 28, 1992, my world shifted when the baby arrived. I just knew that all things good just arrived. She was going to do great things. I could feel it in my bones. I named her Miranda, which means admirable or to be admired. I knew I was perfectly capable of screwing this up, so I prayed hard for her. I prayed that where my parenting skills were lacking, His spirit would make up the difference in making her who *He* wanted her to be.

I figured He would have a lot of slack to make up for, but *He* was faithful and did amazing things. The only way we were surviving was if God had shown up.

To be perfectly honest, I was an eighth-grade dropout and worked for minimum wage. When Miranda was three, her dad left. He came back when she was four and we tried to work it out, but the week before she started kindergarten, he left again—this time for good. Miranda's kindergarten teacher deserves an award. I am pretty sure she had wings she hid under her clothes. A five-year-old doesn't understand being walked away from. Most adults don't even understand it. She sure was a handful.

For a very long time in my life, I was a very square peg trying to fit in a round hole. I didn't fit anywhere. First, I was married at fourteen. Where does that fit in? Does this couple go out with other married couples? There was no one married at my age or even close to my age for a long time. I was pregnant at fifteen. I had a baby at sixteen. I was separated from my husband at nineteen. I was getting a divorce by the time I was twenty-one. By the time I was twenty-two I had lived a lot. It was a very long time before I found a place where I felt like I fit in. I was OK not fitting in, but every now and then I would crave the need to just be normal. If there is such a thing.

Before long, I moved in with my sister, who was also going through a divorce and who had a son. We wanted our kids to at least not be lonely. They grew up thick as thieves. I got a job as a nanny, taking Miranda to work with me. My employers bought me a vehicle, taking payments out of my work check because my ex-husband had left me with the only car we had.

I could quote statistics on how much the odds were stacked against us. I attempted to go to school a couple of times, and it would seem like the odds were simply stacked too high or that it just wasn't time. My sister and I were busy raising our kids and going to work. School was an impossibility, it would seem. I would tuck Miranda in bed and she would say her prayers, and she would pray for a dad and a baby brother. I once asked if she wouldn't prefer a baby sister, but she was adamant. It had to be a boy.

One Sunday morning, I was rushing to church. I was supposed to be the one serving as hostess and was running late so I threw my hair in a bun and made it to the church just in the nick of time. After all, who did I have to impress? Wouldn't you know, in walks the best-looking man I have ever seen in my life. He would later tell me that after service that day, when my daughter and I walked away, he looked over at his sister and said, "Don't be surprised if I am that little girl's daddy someday." Turns out he was right. We were married on

November 15, 2001. By August 2002, I had given birth to a beautiful baby boy. And shortly thereafter, God showed me that I *was never* alone.

I was twenty-six when I gave birth to my son. He was and still is perfection in my sight. I went into labor on a Saturday and had him on Sunday. We went home on Tuesday. Thursday morning, I woke up and couldn't really breathe. I called my husband and asked him to come home and take me back to the hospital. I was sure it wasn't anything big, but I had this nagging feeling that made me think I needed to check. Something was telling me to go even though I just left the hospital. It was the last place I wanted to be or to take my new baby.

We arrived and I was being a chatty Cathy as the triage nurse called me back to check me in. Adam and four-day-old Jess were sitting in the waiting room until I told him to take the baby and run and grab a haircut because we were close to where he got his hair cut while they checked me out. I was sure it was no big deal. She was a really great nurse and as we were talking, she took my blood pressure. I noticed the numbers come up on the screen of the machine as 199/100. I had just spent three days in the hospital having it checked constantly so I knew that was off. I said something along the lines of, "Whoa. Is that really my blood pressure?" The nurse was still very nice, but something changed. She took my pulse and very politely left the room for a second. When she came back, she had a wheelchair and told me to get in, in a tone of voice that let me know, if she were my mother, she would have added "*Now*" to the end of that sentence. My pulse was very low.

She put me in a bed and a doctor came in shortly and examined me. I heard him call the maternity ward and ask about my pregnancy and delivery. It was a textbook pregnancy, so it was a very short call. They gave me a diuretic. The nurse came back five minutes later asking if I needed to go to the bathroom. Nope. She came back again. Nope. The third time she came back when I told her no, she told me to yell when I was ready to go to the bathroom. I am not even going to lie. Five minutes later, I had to go to the bathroom to take the world's longest pee break. It seemed like I peed for twenty minutes. I wanted to yell from the bathroom, "Something is wrong here, I am still peeeeiingggg!!"

After I spent a small lifetime in the bathroom, a tech came to get me and take me up to do an ultrasound on my heart. At this point, I just assumed they were doing what needs to be done so I could go home. As she was performing the procedure she asked, "So, have you had heart problems before?" Um. No. Why? "Well, they are admitting you for congestive heart failure." I have never in my life gone from serene and content to tears coming down my face instantaneously.

You know, you feel tears coming on. It's not normal to go from one to the other without something happening in between, but that is exactly what happened. She took me back down to the emergency room. I cannot begin to describe the feelings I had in that moment. Alone. Scared. Panicked. As a nurse walked by, I asked for a phone and called my husband. I called and told him they were admitting me for congestive heart failure, so he and the baby came rushing back to the hospital. I was given a room and the doctor on call came to see me. He was going to be running a bunch of tests the next day and would be monitoring me overnight. We had just had Jess so Adam's entire family was up from North Carolina. After my best friend showed up, I told Adam to take the baby home. We were all exhausted.

My BFF stayed until she could no longer hold her eyes open and I finally told her she could go home too. I asked her to open the blinds on the window so I could see outside, and she left. It was raining outside and I remember thinking, *That's about right. It matches my day.* I was utterly alone and I was scared. I was afraid to go to sleep because I was afraid, I wouldn't wake up. I called a friend of mine around 1 a.m., crying. I told her I didn't want to die, and she prayed for me. She stayed on the phone until past 3 a.m., when I could no longer stay awake. The next thing I remember, a nurse was coming in to monitor things and check on me; it was still dark. Shortly after that, I woke up to sunshine streaming through the window and thinking, *I made it.* They ran all kinds of tests on my heart. The doctor looked at the ultrasound. He scheduled a follow-up visit.

I left the hospital thinking I had been abandoned by God. After all, my mom was the piano player at the church I grew up in. I slept under church pews as a kid. I have always felt God there, right beside me, getting me through life. But that night, the only thing I felt was fear. I could not feel Him. I felt abandoned. I felt like an orphan. I went back to the doctor thirty days later and was cleared by the doctor. But that feeling of constant loneliness never went anywhere. I would go to church. I would read the Bible. I would pray and sing. Nothing.

Three months after that doctor visit, I was working behind the counter at the bakery I managed, once again being a chatty Cathy with my customer. We started talking about our kids and I mentioned my new little baby and then what happened afterwards. She told me she was a nurse in the cardiovascular care unit at a local hospital. She asked me very seriously if I were OK and proceeded to tell me what it's called when you go into heart failure after having a baby. It's called postpartum cardiomyopathy, of which there is no cure. She told me she lost a patient that week after she had waited for a heart transplant for twelve years after being diagnosed. She told me she was so happy that I was OK. She was very sincere and very kind.

I will never forget finishing my shift and going to my car. I can still remember the moment I shut my car door, the sound of the door coming closed, the spirit of the Lord filling my car. And God spoke to my heart in that moment, "I never left you. I was there the whole time. You should've known that." I could finally see the miracles that happened during those three months. Not being a hospital person but going anyway after having a nagging voice that I should have it checked out. The head of cardiology being the doctor on call for that weekend. Losing pound after pound of fluid overnight, twenty-five-ish, I think it was. Admitted to the hospital one day for heart failure and getting released the *next day*. A nurse that worked in a cardiovascular care unit at a hospital, spelling it out for me on my job after I had moped around for three months letting fear mess with my head and my heart. Those black letters on that white page I had read all my life changed for me that day, and I lived to tell you. You are not alone. Ever.

I often look over my life and reflect on the girl that I was. I look at my daughter's life and I am blown away by what God did with what little I gave him. My daughter is now twenty-seven. She has worked alongside members of Congress in Washington, D.C., fighting for religious freedom around the world. Her eyes have seen things I may never see. She helped install water filters in homes with dirty water on a mission's trip to the Dominican Republic. She has traveled to Poland, Jordan, and Israel with the Philos Project, a small U.S.-based academic group that studies the three major monotheistic religions in the world and how to help relations among Jews, Muslims, and Christians. She loves justice and she is a defender of those weaker than herself. She continues working in D.C., now for a nonprofit that promotes economic growth and opportunity through the tax code, while she attends law school.

As for me, when my son was about two years old, I got a call from a relative telling me to go to school and finish my education, so I decided why not? I registered for classes and started going. I'm not going to sugarcoat it and tell you it was easy because other than losing my parents, it was the hardest thing I have ever done. After earning my GED, I went on to get an associate degree at a local community college that allowed me to transfer in as a junior to Virginia Commonwealth University (VCU), and by 2009 I had my BA in history. It is one thing to graduate from school. It is another thing to be an eighth-grade dropout standing in the Richmond (Virginia) Coliseum and getting your degree in front of your kids and husband. If there ever was a perfect day in my life, that was one of them. The weather held off so we could have a BBQ, and my favorite people were there; some came from as far away as Ohio and California. And my husband and kids got to see what perseverance and hard work looks like.

I just want to point out that I have never attended high school a day in my life. For my sixteenth birthday, my sister, Jackie, handed me a check made out to the adult education system for Chesterfield County, Virginia. I was bummed. I actually had the audacity to complain that my gift could have been something I could have spent on myself. She patted me on the back and simply said, "You will thank me later." (Thanks, Jack!) I drove down and took the test without studying. I figured the worst that could happen was that I could fail. I wouldn't be losing any money. Six weeks later, I got my results. I had passed my high school equivalency exam!

After graduating from VCU, I knew if I stopped going to school, I wouldn't get started again, so I kept going. Time was going to pass anyway, so I might as well pass it in school. By 2012, I had earned my master's degree. If there ever was a story of impossibilities, a story of improbabilities, my life is that story. And yet, here I stand all these years later with a life that I handed to God as ashes, and in return, He gave me something beautiful. I know this. Who am I to say what the value of a life can be? Who am I to know which little human is going to be born with grit and prevail regardless of circumstances? When I look back, I realize that life comes with struggles. It just does. Wealthy, poor, black, white, male, female, young, and old. Life is hard sometimes. We have to realize that some of the most wonderfully unexpected things come through brokenness and hard places. You see, God has never called us to understand. Humanity hates that. I hate that. He does call us to trust.

Proverbs 3:5–6 "Trust in the LORD with all thine heart; and lean not unto thine own understanding. In all thy ways acknowledge him, and he shall direct thy paths." The Word literally tells us *to not* understand.

When I was around thirteen, I went swimming at a rock quarry. It was a very long trail to get to the bottom where the water was. The fastest way was to jump. But gracious, it was such a long way down. Every teenager on the edge of that ledge started talking at once about who was going to jump first. I listened to the bickering back and forth for a second and then, without thinking, I took off running. It was such a high ledge that I remember thinking about halfway down that I should have hit the water by now. I hit the water and scraped my leg from the hip almost to the knee. I could've been killed. I am still here and I lived to tell the tale.

When we trust in the Lord with all our hearts and we learn to "lean not to our own understanding," as

Proverbs 3 instructs us, we are like my blind faith that day on the cliff. We just jump. We know that whatever happens on the other side of that cliff, it's alright because God is on the other side. No worries. Hakuna Matata.

Bella

I have always been a preacher's kid, so when I got to college, that pressure was off and I could go wherever I wanted and do what I wanted. However, my pregnancy came as a result of my brokenness. I was at school, depressed, and feeling like I had nothing. I had been hurt and betrayed by a lot of people there. I had this guy that I liked. We weren't boyfriend and girlfriend—we just liked each other. Whatever it was, I decided it wasn't healthy and broke it off. It made him very bitter and very angry. We ran in the same circles, so when I went to a party and I knew he was going to be there, I told my friends that I didn't want to be near him while we were there. He had gone off on me the week before and said some horrible things. He hated me.

A week later, I went to a party and drank heavily that night. I passed out and when I woke up, I felt gross and I was in pain. I thought, *Why do I feel like this?* I remembered that my ex was at that party and I thought, *If someone did something to me, it was probably him.* I had his number, so I texted him and asked him if something happened, and he said yes.

I asked why he would do something like that to me. I asked why he would think something like that was OK. His reply to me was it was my own fault for getting that drunk. I didn't know what to do. I asked myself if it was my fault because I got drunk. I wasn't even sure if something really happened until he laughed at me over the text and acted like I was a joke. He said such degrading things to me. I felt broken and wasn't sure anyone would believe me, or if they would just think I got drunk and had sex with him—which I would never do after breaking up with someone.

I felt so dirty and so empty. I was confused. I was in such shock, and the friends I thought I had, turned out to not really be my friends. Except for one guy. Lucas noticed something was wrong with me, so I told him. He was angry and wanted to fight the guy, but I begged him to leave it alone; I didn't want him to get in trouble for fighting, so we left it alone. A few weeks later, I was internalizing all that had happened and reflecting on my first serious relationship. He was always pressuring me even when I told him I didn't want to do this or I didn't want to do that. I realized that any physical relationship that I had ever had was with someone overpowering me or someone taking advantage of me.

I decided that I wanted to be the one deciding what happened. I wanted it to be with someone that I cared about and with someone that cared about me. That's how things escalated with Lucas. I was thinking that I wanted my power back. I wanted to be the one to choose. Sure enough, I got pregnant. It was overwhelming to go from one extreme to another. What in the world was I going to do? I was not in a good place. I felt broken. I felt like I was in the deepest pit I had ever been in and I didn't know how to get out. I was embarrassed. I didn't want to tell my parents about it.

I found out I was pregnant because it was the holidays and we were eating a lot of bad food, so when I got sick, I thought it was all the bad food we were eating. Fast-forward to the day after New Year's. We went out to eat after church and I just felt so full. Like abnormally full. Afterward, I decided I was going to get a test. I headed over to the store with Lucas and my BFF to buy four of those tests that say "pregnant" or "not pregnant." As I looked over all four of the tests, they all said "pregnant." We were all shocked. I walked back to the car and I started bawling and bawling. I kept saying over and over again, "I can't do this. I can't do this. I can't do this." I was not where I was supposed to be. I was so broken and so hurt. I was just trying to work through my own stuff. I didn't want to do this. Lucas was in school and I was going to uproot his life, too. I just couldn't do this.

Lucas calmly told me, "We will figure it out, Bella. We will figure it out."

It was horrible.

My friend took me to a place in Richmond that did a free pregnancy test, as well as an ultrasound if you tested positive—just to confirm that all those pregnancy tests were right. They talked to me about my options. They were godly women. They talked to me about God. They prayed with me. They encouraged me that I was going to be OK. That life is beautiful and that there were other options if I kept the baby. But I knew if I kept it, I was going to raise it. I wasn't far enough along to do the ultrasound that visit, so Lucas took off work and we got our first ultrasound together. We both cried.

He told his dad about it first. Lucas wanted to hear it from a man's point of view. His dad told him that it was OK and that he could do it. He told him to have the baby and be happy. He was very encouraging. He wanted to be a grandpa.

It made me a little more at peace, but I knew I wasn't going to get the same thing at home. My friend Regina was another big encourager. I told her that I didn't want an abortion, but that she didn't understand how much this was going to hurt my parents. I had always tried to make them happy, and I did not want to do this to them.

She was blunt. She told me, "There's always another way."

I came back with, "There is no other way."

Her reply? "You shouldn't terminate a pregnancy just because it's going to hurt someone's feelings. That's dumb. I love you, but I won't support you in that."

The first person in my family that I told was my sister. I decided to tell my family over the weekend after the second ultrasound, so when I texted her and asked if she was coming home, she called me. She was suspicious that I asked about her coming home. I told her I just wanted to talk to the fam about stuff going on in my life. She wanted to know exactly what stuff, so when I told her the changes I was going to be making for my future, she asked me point-blank if I was pregnant. She cried.

When I finally sat my parents down to tell them, and I couldn't get the words out, my mom said it for me. My father asked if it was some kind of joke. He really thought we were playing a trick on him. My sister, in a feeble attempt to save me, told them not to be too hard on me because of what had happened to me at the party and at school. My dad went for a long walk to think. He had been hit with everything I had been going through all at once. When he came back from his walk, my sister, my mom, and I were looking at the ultrasound pictures. When I asked if he wanted to see them, he said yes. But then when he saw them, he started to cry. And it was upsetting. I wasn't due for a while, so we had some time to adjust. We spent a lot of time communicating and being there for one another. My dad got to see the consistency of Lucas. That helped. He wasn't just a guy that got me pregnant, but he was a man that really cared and wasn't going anywhere. It was a hard adjustment, trying to balance celebrating a new life; my dad was a pastor, and being a pastor's daughter who was pregnant and not married was not OK. But we talked through a lot of it.

My mom encouraged me to go to a counselor to get emotionally prepared for a baby, which I did. My church was very kind to me and if anything bad was said, it didn't get back to me. Other people may have made comments, but the church was good to me.

When Asher was finally born, any kind of negativity, hurt, or pain was gone. He was such a happy baby. I *knew* my parents would love him. I have loved watching Asher grow. I have taken tons of pictures. Having Asher saved me. I don't like asking for help, so I wouldn't have if not for Asher. I would still be in college trying to figure out how to get out of that pit I was in. Getting pregnant forced me to get the help I needed for myself. I wouldn't go back and change things.

Lucas and I talk about how this little baby that is so sweet and so fun would have been gotten rid of. Asher makes us so happy now. I wouldn't take back anything. If not for Asher, I probably would have kept friend-zoning Lucas instead of committing to this great guy and this great relationship. He is so great and Asher is so great. Even though it wasn't ideal and I wanted to be a young adult longer and enjoy just focusing on myself and doing whatever I wanted with no responsibilities, I wouldn't trade it. It has been a transition and an adjustment, but I am happier than I have ever been in my life, and I am more secure. I feel grounded and I feel that God has worked things out and directed my path.

I have always wanted to bless others and minister to others, but having Asher in my life makes me want to be better. I think about him first and others before myself. It's crazy and my schedule is full, but I love it.

CHAPTER 5

The Post–Abortion Experience: Reflecting on the Past

Savannah* • Emma*

Savannah

I was raised in a Christian family in which premarital sex was a big sin. I went off to college and stopped going to church as much. I was having fun with friends, drinking, and partying. Everyone was having sex around me, and when I started dating a guy, it ended up evolving into a sexual relationship.

I had gotten a little casual about sex, you could say. It was something I did pretty quickly with my boyfriend. I don't think at that time that I was seeing premarital sex for what it was, or the impact that it had or could have on me. John was a boyfriend I had after college. I dated him in my mid-twenties. He was a guy I liked and was in a relationship with, but it was a fair-weather relationship. It was carefree and we were both OK walking away from each other if things got hard. We were committed, but not necessarily looking for a future together. We were just having a lot of fun together. I had met his family; he had met mine. But again, it was nothing serious. Neither one of us were at a point where we were ready to settle down.

I was a manager at a college and I was at the beginning of my career; it had kind of taken off a bit. My period was late, so I went and got a pregnancy test. I was going to test in the bathroom at work. That's how casual I was about it. I was not thinking I was actually pregnant. I was thinking I would take this test and it would tell me I was not pregnant to ease my nerves. And it came up positive.

It was the weirdest feeling. There was nothing happy in me at all. I can't put into words how I felt in that moment, except I was very scared. I called John and I told him. And his reaction was much like mine. Stunned. The more we thought about it, the more it compounded into all the things that wouldn't be possible. Looking back now, as a forty-year-old woman, all of my friends have children. Children are the natural progression in life. It is a natural thing. But at that time, none of that occurred to me. I had this situation that I had not planned on. The first thing I thought about was shaming my parents and their church. That thought came to me in that bathroom stall at work that day. I said to myself: *I will shame my parents and that church.* They have been so active and perfect. Now they are going to have to face all these people with a daughter that is unmarried and pregnant. That was the first thing I thought.

The second thing that went through my mind was that I would never be able to afford a babysitter. My parents could disown me; looking back now, I know they never would have, but at that time, I thought that if they did, I would never have been able to manage this on my own. I thought, *I won't be able to afford a babysitter. I don't have this huge family that will gather around me to help.* Looking back, I know I would have had help. My parents would have *loved* this child. John's parents would have loved this child. Since then, several of John's nieces have been born. His family dotes on those girls. Their lives center around these children.

John very simply asked me, "Savannah, do you plan to travel to Europe? Do you want to get your master's degree? You need it to survive out here. Have you started putting away money for a college fund for a child? Are you prepared for this?" He really put it very bluntly to me, to the point of cruelty. The way he said those things let me know that he was not on board at all. There would be no talking him into this thing. Looking back, we were both from wealthy families. I had a great job. We were in a pretty good position financially.

I did have one girlfriend come talk to me that told me to think about it for a minute. "You will have a baby. You will find a babysitter."

I was never drawn to her side. The fear kept ruling my decision-making. It was the next day that I made the appointment. It was so easy to get this done. John accompanied me to the appointment. We sat in the waiting room. No one was talking. Everyone was watching the television.

I got called back by a nurse who was neutral. She could have been a statue. She made sure I understood I was in a position to have a baby. That if I wanted to have a baby, I could handle it. When she said that, for a moment I latched onto it. I felt like if I had an advocate in there that was against abortion I would have *absolutely* gone in that direction. I was scared to talk with anyone that was not for abortion because I knew my mind probably would have been changed. When she said that, I was not sure I wanted to go through with it. She said, "Why don't I go get your boyfriend?"

He came in with the expression on his face that said, "What's the problem? What is the holdup here? What do you want to talk about?"

"I don't know." I told him I just didn't know if this was the right decision.

I just remember looking up and both of them just looking at me in that way. Like, *really, you're wasting our time.* Waiting for something to happen. Waiting for me to figure out I was just wasting time. Which made me falter in my hesitation.

"OK, I am ready. I *am* ready."

The nurse started repeating to me, "You are, you're ready. OK. You're ready. OK. Then I will be right back."

John and I sat there looking at each other like *OK.*

The nurse came in with a pill and a glass of water, which she handed to me. I looked at both of their faces. Back and forth, and then I finally popped the pill.

She told me that in two days, I was going to cramp really badly; she gave me hydrocodone for pain. John and I left and went out to dinner, where I drank very heavily. I drank so much and was really sad and angry at him. It was just this empty, scary feeling.

I had taken two days off work so I could get through the process. I started having symptoms and it was very painful. It was not this easy thing that they made it out to be. It was very, very painful. I did not want anyone around me. I did not want anyone to call me. It was just a very painful period of time. Painful on so many levels. Physically and emotionally. The following week, I was just sort of a zombie.

I am not sure if I have blocked it out or if it has been so long, eleven or twelve years, but one of my best friends was married and pregnant at the same time. Now, every time I see her daughter, I always know that's how old my daughter would have been. And I say daughter because years after the abortion, John told me that he and his mother went out to Chinese the evening after the abortion and he got a fortune cookie. On one side was his fortune, and on the other side, the word "daughter," so I always thought it was a girl.

Looking back now, I know that it started me down a long road of addiction. I was very numb for a long time. I started taking antidepressants and pills for pain when I didn't have pain. It would give me a buzz that made me feel OK. There was never a grieving process, but I numbed myself for years. It became a lifestyle for me. I ended up being a drug addict. I ended up getting fired from three very good jobs for issues ultimately related to drug addiction. I went through unsuccessful relationship after unsuccessful relationship—a total of six. I never had a desire for a family after that. Even now, the thought of having a child is too painful for me. I don't know, but I imagine how special being a mother is, and it scares me. I am scared that it will make me a mess.

Regarding the areas of your life that an abortion affects as you grow and have families, I have talked to women that had an abortion and then had children. It makes them grieve and realize the magnitude of what they did. And then there are women who never have children and always think about it. I won't say daily, but it is there always. You grieve with children and you grieve without them. You can't get away from the grief. I have talked with the women that, after having a baby, cannot believe they made the other choice for their other pregnancy. They look at the child they have and all that child has brought to their life.

Sometimes, I have anger toward women whose whole life revolves around their kids because I don't have that. When you don't have children, you have to find other things to fill your life. I will tell you that none of those other things has ever fulfilled me like I know my friend's children fulfill them. You always have a longing because you are not experiencing the life-changing event of having children. Every time you hear a woman say that they couldn't imagine their life without their child, you think about how your life *could* have been.

You meet people that have very strong views one way or the other; it's very hard to be around very opinionated people because you don't want to feel like a bad person, and you know what you did. It's a shameful thing and secrets keep you sick. It's a secret you want to keep a secret. When I hear of other women having abortions, it eerily comforts me. It makes me feel like I am not that bad of a person. It is an ongoing loneliness for me. Another way it has affected me includes my relationship with my parents. It affected them. They don't have any grandchildren.

I was in a very sad place one time. I was going through a bad breakup and my mother came over to be with me. In an attempt to comfort me, she said (as I was crying hysterically over the breakup), "Savannah, do you know what is really sad? I just got back from a church retreat where a friend told me that she was a grandmother of four, three that are alive. Her daughter had an abortion. That's something to be sad about."

When she said that, I just could no longer hold it from her. I never told her that the first thought that came to my mind when I found out I was pregnant was shaming them at their church. Ever since then, when there is a child around (which is usually my friends' kids or my mom's friends' grandkids) there is an uncomfortableness with my family. I never told my dad; I knew my mom would share it with him because they share everything. He and I have cried about it together but never actually spoke the words about what happened.

I always knew abortion was a sin before my abortion. Looking back objectively on my abortion (fifteen years later), my greatest fears at that time were money and shaming my parents; I know now that without a doubt, money would not have been an issue. At all. After getting to know my parents for who they really are and not who I thought they were back at that time, I know they would have rallied around me. I have seen many people in worse situations than myself. It is so very possible. I think having a baby is overwhelming to anyone.

I have a friend that had an abortion in high school. Later, when she'd only been dating a guy for three weeks and she found out she was pregnant, she told him she would never have an abortion again and that she was having that baby. He responded with a simple OK, and then they went to her grandmother's house and had a talk with her grandma. Her grandma told them to get married and have a baby! They had nothing and hardly knew each other. They went on to have two more babies for a total of three girls. *They made it work.* They have three college-educated daughters. He made $17,000 as a farmer and she stayed at home. They did *fine!* I see John with his nieces and he would have made a fine father. He has never been able to have a successful relationship either all these years. We would have been fine.

When we see each other, we never talk about what we did; the night that it happened was so dark for us. When we went out, we spent the night talking about all the horrible things that had happened to us. All the bad things.

It went downhill from that point. A part of my soul was so heavy. I had injured a part of my soul. It was a trigger that led to drug addiction. They gave me pain medicine after the abortion that made me numb. I could take hydrocodone and Xanax together and be numb. I was a partier, and pre-abortion, alcohol was for having a good time. Post-abortion, alcohol and drugs were self-medication. It was a way of not having to feel, well, anything. The hurt was numbed but so were the joy and happiness that come with life because addiction numbs everything. So, you miss out. I do know that you can get joy back and you can come back from addiction. At one point, I recognized that I hid it; I knew it was a problem. I didn't just need to detox, but I needed a support system to help me get off medications. I went to rehab and I worked through the addiction. The only thing I am currently on is an antidepressant.

I am forty-one now, but if I could talk to the twenty-five-year-old version of myself, I would tell her simply that I don't *know* what your life would be like if you had the baby, but I do know what your life would be like if you don't. And you are going to have a lot of really painful times ahead of you, maybe even a whole life of pain. And all the obstacles you thought were obstacles were not obstacles at all. My parents would have been the best grandparents.

The thought of not having to live with all this is really cool. You live with this your whole life. If I could give any advice to a girl facing an unplanned pregnancy, I would tell her to go talk to a woman that has had an abortion and then go talk to a woman that has not. There is a difference.

Emma

My boyfriend and I got engaged; I was nineteen at the time. He got a scholarship to go to a university he really wanted to go to and wanted me to move there with him as his girlfriend. I told him I wouldn't do that without being married. Meanwhile, I missed my cycle and I wasn't feeling normal, so my friend and I went to a clinic and got a pregnancy test. It was positive. I was devastated and scared. My boyfriend and I were not very sexually active because I didn't believe in having sex before marriage. We might be together once every six months. Which is why I was in such shock that I didn't tell him for about three weeks—to give myself time to process it all. I wanted to figure out what I was going to do.

I finally told him after almost a month. I thought he was going to be more positive about it, to be honest. He was shocked, sad, and it made him depressed. His first response, after the shock wore off, was to tell me to get rid of it. We had nothing to offer a baby. We had no money and he had to finish school. I was working but living at home and he was rooming at college.

We argued when I told him I wanted to keep it. He became very distant and withdrawn. I told him I could keep it and raise it on my own, and he continued to tell me to get rid of it. When I told my family, the response from my mom and siblings wasn't positive either, which reinforced what he was saying to me. In fact, I only had one person that said something even remotely positive about the pregnancy. My brother's girlfriend told me that it was my body and if I wanted to have the baby, I could. She told me not to let anyone force me to do anything.

My boyfriend was still adamant. After a while, I started to believe him when he said we had nothing and could offer nothing. I became hopeless. From the time I told him that I was pregnant to the time I relented and had an abortion was about two weeks. I made the appointment to get the abortion and he picked me up in a taxi. I remember looking out the back window of the taxi on the ride to the facility and I cried all the way to the abortion clinic, which was about a thirty-minute drive.

We checked in and sat amongst other girls waiting. Finally, a nurse came and took me back to the room. I remember asking her if this was a baby a couple of times. She told me there was nothing formed and it was just a blob of tissue. She didn't convince me. I already felt like it was something I had to do. They called me back and put me on the table. The tears started until I was sobbing so hard by the time the doctor came in that he told the nurses that he could not do it. They made me get off the table and go into another room to calm down. The nurse finally came in and rather sternly told me the doctor wasn't going to do the procedure if I didn't stop crying. It took me about ten or fifteen minutes to calm down enough to get back on the table. The procedure took about twenty minutes. The pain was excruciating, like nothing I have ever felt in my life. They didn't give anything for pain. I felt everything. I remember there was a little sink on the side of the room, and I thought that my baby was in that sink. By the time they took me to the back for recovery, all I could think was that I wanted to die.

We took a taxi home. My boyfriend was very quiet, other than asking if I was OK. I laid on the couch and covered my head. I didn't want to eat or talk and I became very depressed. Once again, my brother's girl-friend showed up and she tried her best to comfort me as much as possible. I do not have the vocabulary to describe the guilt that I felt. I didn't know how to get rid of this feeling, so I started blocking it away and acting like it never happened. My brother's girlfriend was the last person I talked about it with for a long time. About eight months later, I was living with a girl-friend and I was watching the evening news and there was a big abortion protest, and all of sudden all those emotions came back to me. I thought I had tucked them away really well until that moment in front of the news, and when it surfaced, I fell apart on the couch.

I ran to my room and locked myself in. I didn't speak for the rest of the evening. I could hear my roommate talking to someone on the phone; she was confused and didn't understand what happened. I remember being shocked at how tight I thought I had tucked it away inside myself and how hard and fast all those emotions came back. To this day, I know they are still there below the surface. I can hear the word "abortion" and it will touch my heart.

When my roommate cornered me the next day. I confessed what happened to me. She talked me through her experiences of getting pregnant and being a single mom. When you feel like you have no support, she told me you will feel forced to make those choices that are not your own. She encouraged me to ask God for forgiveness and make peace. It was the first time in a long time that I had some inner peace. You can avoid talking about abortion to others, but you cannot deny what has happened to you or what you have done. It was then that I asked God to forgive me and I stopped denying what had happened to myself. And I think that was when my healing began.

About two years later, my boyfriend and I got married. We got pregnant on our honeymoon with our first baby. When I found out I was pregnant, someone told me about a crisis pregnancy center. I had never heard of one before. We still did not have a lot of resources and my husband was still in school, so I went to the crisis pregnancy center for a free pregnancy test.

As I sat there listening to all the stuff they did for women facing an unplanned pregnancy, it occurred to me that those people that put me back on that table sobbing knew about this place, and they didn't even give me the option to call a pregnancy center. I don't feel they were trying to help me. To this day, I believe that in their eyes, I had no value. And if I didn't have value, my baby surely didn't. I sat there at the crisis pregnancy center thinking that it was all about money at the other place. I was just a quick couple of hundred dollars.

For a place that was "helping" me, they didn't even give me the option to make another choice. They didn't tell me, "Maybe you should go to this other center and explore other options there."

I do not believe they are there to help poor girls out, and I know if they did it to me, they did it to other girls and probably still do. If I had been in there with confidence, it would have been one thing, but I was in there in such a mess they had to take me off the table for me to calm myself down.

We were married for a very long time and went on to have three other children. I loved him very much but the truth is, somewhere in the back of my mind was a lack of trust on my part. I thought when push came to shove, he would put his needs and wants first because of what happened with our first pregnancy. The marriage eventually disintegrated from infidelity years later, which only confirmed what I had felt all along.

If I had it to do over again, without a doubt and without hesitation, I would not have chosen abortion. Knowing what I know now, feeling what I feel now, I would not have made that choice. Adoption was not a word mentioned to me. I needed to hear those things at that time. One of the things on my bucket list is to volunteer at one of those pregnancy centers. I will never forget the love they showed me. I will never forget feeling valued.

If I could help a woman now facing the same things I was facing when I got pregnant, I would help her understand that things don't go as planned. God extends mercy in those situations. There are resources. I would tell her that how she feels now will change. You will not feel the same later. I would also let her know that everyone is different and because of that, no one can tell you 100 percent you aren't going to be affected by it. I would plead with them to make a different choice. I know what it does emotionally. If it were one of my daughters or nieces, I would offer to take care of the baby (which I have done before). I would beg, plead, and cry for them to choose something else. Anything else.

CHAPTER 6

The Adoption Option

Gail • Tanya

Gail

I was about twenty-eight years old when I found out I could not have children. My husband and I had been married for about five years and we decided it was time to start a family. I went in for an exploratory type of exam and they let me know that I didn't have primary ovarian deficiency, but that I had no ovaries. There was absolutely no chance of me having a baby. It was hurtful and painful to hear that. It was something everyone else got to do and I wasn't going to get to experience it. It was hard. I was around couples who got married about the same time as my husband and me, and they had babies in their first year of marriage and got to enjoy their babies. Then the day came when we were ready, and I was not going to get to do that. My husband, being the wonderful man that he is, told me that it was going to be OK and that there were children's homes. There were other avenues that we could pursue.

We looked at artificial insemination, but back in the 1980s, it was $15,000 a try and only a forty percent chance that it would work. We didn't have that kind of money. When we checked into adoption, it was $10,000 upfront to adopt a baby. It was $3,000 alone to fill out the application. Again, we did not have that kind of money. There were no payment plans for that sort of thing.

We learned, through my family, of a two-year-old boy whose mother was having a hard time taking care of him. She had been taking him place to place until she ended up at a family member's house telling them that if they knew of someone willing to adopt him, she would gladly love to place him. So, when they called, we immediately went to meet her and her boyfriend. She brought the boy to us with a paper bag of clothes and a couple of toys. She handed him to us and told us we could reach out to an attorney here in town. She said the boy was very loving, but that she was just not a great mother. Kirk and I were so excited. We were looking at this blond-haired, blue-eyed little boy smiling and eating his pizza. We were like, "Is this really happening?" As we were putting him the car, I couldn't help but think that this was too good to be true. We took him to my parents' house, where we had a bed for him. We got up the next morning and we went to an attorney. We signed papers saying that the parents planned to proceed with adoption and placed all medical care and decisions with these two people. Then we brought him home to Hampton, Virginia. It was easy. He never cried or acted like he missed anyone. The clothes in the paper bag were too large for him, so we went out and got him everything he needed. Before long, he was calling us Mom and Dad. The only way to describe him was a little angel.

Every now and again, he would ask where Peachy (his birth mother) was. We would tell him that Peachy was at work. She did not give us a number at which to reach her. She didn't want to be contacted until she had dates lined up for the legal paperwork. After about three months, the phone calls started. She needed to pick him up for an appointment on Friday and wouldn't be back until Monday, but not to worry, she would bring him back to us. We did this about three or four times over the next year. Finally, I started asking why we hadn't heard from the attorney. She gave me the name of her attorney, so I called him and asked how long the adoption proceedings should take. He let me know that the only client he had with the name I mentioned was trying to get child support payments increased. So, her real story was that she had court-ordered child support coming in from the baby's father and it wasn't enough. She had us taking care of her son but would take him to go to the lawyer and get the support raised while she was running out going across the country with a trucker. She was gaming the system. There was no mention of adoption to her attorney. I told the attorney thank you and hung up.

The next time she called, I talked with her about it. She let me know that she was going to adopt him to us regardless. Two months later, we received a call from her saying she had to pick him up because her sister was worried about him. She needed to pick him up and take him to her sister's house so she could see that he was safe. She would talk with her about the adoption and it would all be fine. After that, we didn't trust anything. We clung to him with our hearts but we were preparing ourselves for when she came to get him. It was a killer. We didn't want it to affect him. I didn't want him to know.

She told us the day she was coming to pick him up and she let us know they would be traveling through a couple of different states before going back to their home state of West Virginia. So, we bought a canvas bag and started filling it with toys and books. He hadn't been with her in a while and we wanted to help him be excited about his trip with Peachy, but when she pulled up, she told us she didn't know when they would be back. My husband knew then that they would not be coming back, so we packed up everything that was his. We packed his toys, his bed, his high chair, and his eating utensils. They had a pick-up truck and we filled it with everything that was his. We wanted him to have everything that had been his for eighteen months surrounding him when he got to where he was going.

I don't know how much time passed, but I know the day they pulled out of the driveway, I shut the door, laid on the floor, and cried. I didn't want to see anyone. I didn't want anyone to tell me this was going to be OK or that "God has got this," because we didn't do anything to open this door. We prayed if it was God's will, let it happen. We were not going to chase after her. When he left, I told God, "This was your will?" I was silently bitter.

The day he left, my husband went into the bedroom and called my pastor's wife, who was also my best friend. She came over and when I lifted my head off the floor and saw who it was, I told her I didn't want to talk. She told me it was OK, that she didn't come to talk. She laid on the floor for four hours with me. I heard her praying beside me but it was very quiet. She was just a presence that came to be beside me.

The next few weeks were murder. I didn't want to leave the house. For eighteen months, every day, all day long, everything was Josh—and then suddenly it was nothing. It was over. I didn't know where he was going. I had no control over his life. It was all a lie. If the mother had told us the truth in the beginning, we would have taken him anyway. We would have still filled his life with happiness, but she lied. It was hard.

Three months later, I decided I was going to go find him. I needed to know he was OK. I went to West Virginia. I knew some of the family members. I went to their house. I knocked on their doors. After about three doors, I was told that he was living with his aunt and uncle down the road. I finally knocked on their door and tried to explain who I was and what connection I had with Josh. They closed their door all but an inch. They were scared of me. They told me they didn't know me and they didn't know what connection I had with Josh. They didn't know anything about him staying with me for eighteen months. And all of a sudden, Josh came running around the corner and said, "Hey! That's my mommy!" The woman really got scared. Long story short, he was OK, all the toys we bought him were everywhere, and his portrait we had taken was hanging on the wall. This couple raised him until he was about fifteen years old. Peachy called him and wanted him to come live with her, which he did. He ended up having some very rough times in his life after he went to live with her. He made some bad choices and got some bad habits. I found him on Facebook not too long ago. I sent him a message that took me two hours to write, but with much tact, I let him know that once upon a time, this is what happened. I sent him a picture of him and my husband and of him in our lives. He was floored. He remembered my husband.

We gave up adopting after that. We decided if ever it was going to happen, someone would have to knock on my door. People came to me and would tell me of babies needing adoption, and I just didn't have it in me to pursue anything. I was not filling out applications. I was not knocking on doors. It would have to come to me. I wasn't looking for the first adoption, so I definitely wasn't going looking for the second one after what happened with the first. My husband and I took a position pastoring what used to be my home church growing up for about eight or nine years after that. I did not want to go there, to be honest. I started praying and the desire to have a baby came back. I had someone come to me and tell me they had some baby stuff they were getting rid of and wanted to know if I was interested, in case we ever adopted someday. One thing they gave me was a small cradle. I went and bought some blankets and a little bear I named Cody-bear. I laid everything in the bassinet with Cody-bear on top. I went out one day and bought a baby dress and I said this is going to belong to Holli Rebecca Cherie Aikey, whoever she is. I brought it home and hung it on the bassinet. At this point, it had been three years since Josh had been taken from our lives.

Three months after I placed the bassinet in the bedroom, the telephone rang. A girl had gotten pregnant. A neighbor had convinced her not to abort the baby. The family was military, so she would be able to have the baby without cost. The neighbor said she would find a family for her family. They all agreed. She called a few states away to someone that knew me. My friend connected me to the mother of this girl. I called and she let me know that we needed to be prepared to take the baby from the hospital in three days or they were going to have to give the state custody when her daughter was released from the hospital.

We had no money. We have no idea how we would get from West Virginia to Arkansas. We called an attorney. The lawyer told us to pay him a thousand dollars to do the paperwork and that we had to get a lawyer there as well, which would be another thousand dollars. Two thousand dollars. We were both working, but our money was covering our expenses and the church's expenses. We had no money. We went to church one night and prayed. We told the church that we had a special unspoken request, that we needed everyone to pray for. We didn't tell the congregation what it was. We didn't tell them about the opportunity and obstacles we were facing, just that God knew all about it. We didn't mention money. We didn't mention the baby. We looked at our thirty-five-person congregation and just asked them to pray with us. That was all.

The next morning, my husband went to the church to check-in and pray before heading over to his other full-time job. He checked the voicemail and a lady had called and left a message. Her son and daughter-in-law went to our church. She said she didn't really attend church but that she believed in God. She said she heard about a special request that was being prayed about and something tugged on her heart. She wanted to meet Kirk at the church that evening to give him a cashier's check for $2,000. She told us it was a gift and that we could not return it or refuse it. In twenty-four hours, we had all the money we needed for both attorneys. I cried.

Our next hurdle was the home study. It was a six-week process that would never be done in time; after all, we only had three days. We called the social service department and they told us that it couldn't be done in less than six weeks, but they did have a girl that had been on maternity leave for six weeks and maybe she would be willing to take the case. We called and told her our story. She told us she could do it in six days. She came to our home for three days in a row. She made us drive to her office three days in a row for interviewing. At that point, she would submit it to the state for processing and try to get it through. We did exactly that. The paperwork was being processed and Holli's due date came and went, and she wasn't born. The next week came and went and she wasn't born. The paperwork still wasn't back. She finally arrived and two days later the paperwork came through. We had our home study! God held her off for two weeks until the six-week home study that only took two weeks was done.

Another issue we had was that state law in the state she was born in prohibited her from leaving the state for two weeks because of old child slavery laws. We didn't have money to drive out there and stay in a hotel for two weeks. We called a church to see if there was someone there that could take care of the baby until we could get there. They connected us to one of their members that ran a childcare center from her home. The woman told us she would be more than happy to go get her and take care of her until we could get there. The family picked her up from the hospital but we had forgotten to tell them what we were going to call her! When we called the next day and told them her name was Holli, they laughed. The night before, they realized the baby didn't have a name, so they had called her Molly, which was pretty close! Our family gathered money together for us to drive out there and pick her up.

We brought her home and she filled our lives with joy and activity. She was born with blonde hair and the biggest blue eyes you have ever seen. She is outgoing and friendly and has always been that way. She is giving and loyal to her friends. She definitely kept us busy and always kept us on our toes. She was and is a blessing to our parents, her grandparents. I cannot imagine our life without her.

If I could tell her birth mother anything, it would be "Thank you for choosing life." I would tell her that I truly hope that there has not been much pain in knowing that you gave life to someone, a human being that you have never met. I hope that she has not looked back and had deep hurtful regrets because Holli has been well-loved; she and her mother were an answer to our prayers and we have lived our lives loving her and raising her.

Tanya

I grew up in Howard County, Maryland. As a kid, I bounced all over Howard County. I grew up in a very dysfunctional household. My parents were both deaf, so I had to do a lot of the communicating for them when it came to adult phone calls. Needless to say, I grew up very quickly. By the time my youngest sister was born, I was eleven years old. I was taking care of my siblings as well as myself because this was around the time my mother left us for good, leaving us with our father. By the time I was thirteen, my parents were divorced. My father abused me in every way imaginable: physically, emotionally, and sexually. There was a good family that took us three girls in during the week to help my father out—which was so nice!

By the time I was sixteen, I spent my time during the week looking ahead to the weekend so I could run with my friends. I had a boyfriend, but my dad was always interfering with all my relationships. Even my girlfriends. He would do weird things so they would not be allowed back over. I broke up with my boyfriend and just after my seventeenth birthday I found out I was pregnant. I called my ex-boyfriend to tell him I might be pregnant, and his first response was, "You're going to get an abortion, right?"

At that point, I told him, "Absolutely not! I don't believe in that and it's not what I want to do." I didn't know what I was going to do but I wasn't expecting that as his response. I hadn't told my then-current boyfriend yet and I was afraid I was going to lose him. I asked my ex not to tell anyone so that my current boyfriend wouldn't find out from anyone but me. We lived in a small community and we all knew each other.

My ex-boyfriend called his best friend, who lived close to my boyfriend, and of course, told him that I was pregnant with another guy's baby. We didn't have cell phones, so I was rushing to get to my boyfriend to tell him myself. But it took twenty minutes. I pulled in and saw my ex's friend walking away—and I knew. My boyfriend already knew. I could see it.

I was sure it was over. I was crying as I got out of the car. I was heartbroken. I walked over and I told him. He told me it was OK. And that we were going to work through it, and he was really glad I told him and didn't keep it a secret.

I went to my best friend's mom and she took me to a pregnancy center. We got a pregnancy test to confirm everything. I was shown a video on childbirth and one on abortion. Even though it had crossed my mind, I knew I wasn't doing abortion. My dad had old pamphlets about abortion laying around the house when I was young. I knew what it looked like, but it had crossed my mind. I was a Christian, I already believed in God, I was surrounded by Christ's love—and it still crossed my mind. I found out in time to get an abortion and I had time to think about it, but I already knew it was not going to be my choice.

My new boyfriend and I planned on parenting this baby, which terrified me. I was already taking care of my two little sisters; I didn't know what I was doing. I was just a kid. My boyfriend was a few years younger than me, and we were in a new relationship. But we made our decision, and I started hoping and praying that this baby would be a boy. I couldn't protect myself or my sisters from my father, so I needed this baby to be a boy.

With the first sonogram, they couldn't tell me what the sex of the baby was. I thought there was still a chance it could be a boy. After the second sonogram, at around eight months, I found out it was a girl. Panic set in. My dad had led me to believe that if I let certain things happen to me it wouldn't happen to my sisters, which I knew wasn't true. I was seeing the signs. I knew something was happening to them. When I got pregnant, I had confronted my dad and told him to stop. He blamed me, told me it was my fault, told me I didn't want another woman around so I let the abuse happen, and so forth.

I ultimately decided adoption was my best choice. I was presented with a family for the adoption, and I didn't like them. They just weren't the ones. Then the father of the family that had taken care of me during the week when I was younger—a Christian marriage counselor—told me there was a place he knew of that helped with adoption. His wife took me to a local adoption agency, Bethany Christian Services. I sat in there and talked to them. I told them I wanted my daughter to be loved and taken care of. They let me look at three profiles. There was a family in there that I wished my sisters and I could have been adopted by and I thought, since I can't have them for my sisters and myself, why not pick them for my daughter?

I got to deliver my baby with the family that I picked out. She was due on June 19, which is ironic because later, when I did have other children that I was able to parent myself, my next daughter was also due on June 19. But this baby was finally born on July 4, almost two weeks late. It was a sign from God to me not to worry, that I had made the right choice. I felt like I had done what I was supposed to do. She would never be alone as she was independent in the world. That it was OK to let go. Those three days in the hospital, she was all mine. I stayed awake all three days. Other than the nurses taking her for blood work, she was by my side the whole time. I soaked up every single minute, every second with her. And then came time to say my goodbyes. I gave her a little kiss and told her to be good until I got to see her again.

Bethany Christian Services lets you reunite with your baby before they get placed in their adoptive home, if you want. My two sisters had been too young to come to the hospital room, so I wanted that time with them and her. I needed to know she looked good and was OK. When the time came, I didn't get to hold her as much because I wanted my little sisters to meet her and know her, even if only for a day. It took everything I had to not say, "I changed my mind, I want to take her home!" I wanted to take her home. Man, I wanted to take her home so bad, but I knew she wouldn't be safe. Just because I made a bad choice didn't mean she should suffer. She should have a safe home. She did get that. I didn't know for a long time if she did, and that was one of the hardest parts about placing your child in another family.

It's not knowing if your child is OK. Not knowing if your child is hurting. Not knowing if they are being loved, kissed, hugged, with stories being read to them at night. Not knowing if they are being tucked in and told that God loves them. My dad had been adopted and his experience was not as good, so it was a very scary time for me. But God kept telling me this was what was supposed to happen. Every year, I bawled my eyes out on the Fourth of July, but I knew that she was somewhere watching the fireworks too! I knew she was celebrating her day!

Fast-forward thirty-one years to May of 2018. I have a friend with whom I had shared my story privately who begged me to come volunteer with her at a pregnancy center, where I could encourage others and help them see the possibilities of adoption. She told me to come in and see what it was all about. I was uncomfortable telling my story because I didn't know how my daughter was doing, and I needed to know how she was. I prayed with my friend and told her I needed two weeks before I could decide. Three days later, I receive some messages from a Facebook message thread, and my daughter was in that thread.

A cousin that I had never met because she was adopted, had recently had a DNA test done. My daughter's husband, as kind of a joke, gave her a DNA test—and they were a match on Ancestry. My daughter didn't respond to anyone on those sites, but my cousin reached out to her on Facebook. She responded. The day she responded I was going about my life. I pulled up to the gym and there was this song on the radio: "I want you to have it all." And I thought of my daughter and I thought, *I hope you got it.* It was all I ever wanted. I went to work out at the gym and as I was wrapping up and heading to my car there were twenty-two messages for me. I started noticing my birthdate and my ex-boy-friend's birthdate. My mom was on there saying, "That's my daughter." And there was some random person who chimed in with, "Both of my birth mother's parents are deaf." I gasped. I started crying. It was her! I was bawling and trying to get home.

It was happening, God. This was really happening. I asked if I could text when I got home. I was a mess. When I arrived at my house, my first question to my daughter was, "Were you loved and were you taken care of?" She told me she was. Her first question to me was, "Am I a secret?" I told her, without hesitation, absolutely not! I wanted people to know. I wanted people to know that even if you can't have them right there with you in your life, it is still better than other choices. She was never a secret. I asked if she had a good life. She responded, "Yes, because of you." This child is so sweet and amazing. She is a lot like me even though she has not been around me. By July 17, 2018, she was standing in my living room with her husband (also adopted, by the way). By March of 2019, I was in her living room meeting her adoptive parents and seeing where she was raised in Chicago. She took me to her salon and did my hair. I met her older sister who is also adopted.

One of the reasons I chose this family is because they already had a child, a girl that they had adopted three years earlier. They celebrated Adoption Day. I didn't want any secrets for her. I wanted her to always know she was adopted. We sat on the floors and looked at pictures, ate pizza, and played with her nephews. I got to be in the backyard where my daughter played when she was a kid. I was able to see the bedroom she painted when she was a teenager. It was amazing.

That family is amazing. Her parents were so thankful for the gift. I was so thankful for their kindness. They welcomed me in their home and into my daughter's life again, and they didn't have to do that. They have a plaque on the wall for their daughter to read that talks about the gift of adoption. They celebrated Adoption Day while she was growing up. It was a thing like their birthday every year, and every year on my birthday, they prayed for me. By the time my daughter came back into my life, she had such a spirit of gratitude toward me. She knew I was a good person. Her parents made sure she understood the gift of life they were given. All her mother ever wanted to do was be a mother, and she was unable to do so. It was a gift they all received that was priceless.

If I could tell that younger version of myself anything, it would be, "You did a good job." I never thought I would see my daughter again in this life. My best advice for someone in the position I was once in would be to abstain from sex, but if you don't and you find yourself pregnant, choose life.

CHAPTER 7

The Teen and Young Mothers' Guide: Walking with Poise

Dear Young Mama,

The longer I live, the more I know that there are plenty of people that live a life that wouldn't be considered "normal." My hope is that if you have found yourself a teen mom or a mom in her early twenties, that you finish this book with confidence and fresh resolve to run the race set before you. If you have made it through the considerably difficult task of telling your parents, bravo! If you have decided to form an adoption plan or keep and raise your child, bravo! I believe in you. I know you don't realize this, in the midst of the struggle of being a young mother, but you are so much stronger than you know. God has put the good stuff in you. He knew you so well. He knew the decisions you would make before you made them. You will make mistakes on this journey and you will fail. If no one has told you yet, life is like an ocean, and guess what? Any ship's captain will tell you that smooth seas never make skilled sailors. It is rough seas that make a captain an expert seaman.

I have put together some steps to help you navigate this season in your life. And it is a season. Time is going to fly by and you will one day be looking up at that baby boy or girl instead of down. I want it to be a beautiful season for you, not a hardship. If you choose life for your child, I want it to be a good one, not just for him or her, but for you! Looking back over my life,

I wish someone had mapped it out for me or given me the advice I am giving you.

#Need to Know: Put God First and You Will Not Regret It!

I found myself a young single mom, stressed out beyond measure, wondering if I had done anything right as I sat in church. The pastor's wife was talking about the order of things. She had a chart that showed Jesus leading the way, and then the husband and the wife, the kids, and so forth. She went on to explain that if you have found yourself in a situation where there is no husband, you just keep following Jesus. My then six-year-old daughter leaned over to the kid next to her and whispered, "That's what my mom did." I sat back in my seat with the world exactly the way it was before she said it, but I *felt His* hand on my shoulder, and I almost heard Him say, "We've got this."

The first way to take control of your situation, no matter your age, is to run to the Rock! (And I am not referring to Dwayne Johnson.) The outcome depends on you and you alone, and the journey is going to happen regardless of what you decide. The first scenario (with the not-Dwayne-Johnson Rock) is a road paved with miracles. I am not talking about little things, but the most unpredictable surprises that will knock your socks off! The second road is harder and can be done through sheer tenacity, but you will miss so many unexpected beautiful miracles along the way.

The great big God of the universe specializes in the impossible. I used to tell God all the time that He was going to have to make up the difference from where my parenting skills stopped. Even as a young girl, I knew that I only had one shot at raising my daughter and I knew there was no such thing as a perfect parent. I wanted her to become the person that *God* wanted her to become. I dedicated her as a baby and *asked Him* for His help. He heard this young mother's cry and answered my prayers, for which I am eternally grateful. Invite Him into your mess and see what He does!

#Need to Know: Get a Support System in Place.

Many times, this will be your family. I pray you have a good one that loves you unconditionally, but sometimes that is not the case. If it is not, I have some suggestions for you. First, a mentor is a good place to start. If you don't have one, get one. A person that is where you want to be someday. Someone that displays excellent character. Second, find other people that are in your situation—and have your drive and tenacity—and start a group. Exchange numbers and learn to depend on each other. Exchange babysitting dates so you can get a break and so they can get a break. Babysit each other's children while you are in class, one of you choosing night classes and one of you choosing day.

Some of my closest friends to this day are the women that were in my life when I was a single mother. Our kids are grown or almost grown. Some of us have become grandparents. (I find it so funny to be writing that sentence at thirty-nine years old!)

One of these women told me a while back, "Sarah, you did it!"

I asked what I did.

She said, "Remember when we were all single moms and you said you were going to go back to school and get your degree? You did it!"

I forget her sometimes, that girl who was determined to get out of her mess and do something with her life. But my support system reminded me that day.

I recently came across an old home video of our house during this time. The noise level was insane. I actually said, "Wow! That was so chaotic." But at the time, it was my kids, my sister's kids, and our friend's kids. It was a typical Friday night, and we were having a blast. Our kids were laughing and romping around together. I am sure it seemed like a big slumber party to them; they had no clue it was done out of necessity. My daughter and my sister's son grew up like brother and sister, not cousins. They even look a little alike! I didn't feel too sorry for myself back then, but every now and again I would ask, *Why me?* Looking back now, I have such sweet, sweet memories of that time.

I woke up one morning to my nephew jumping up and down on my bed, shouting, "There's a lizard outside, there's a lizard outside!" I rolled over trying to figure out what on earth he could be talking about—a giant dinosaur, maybe? Meanwhile, he was still jumping up and down and yelling. I had to get up and look. I made it to the front door, with him dragging me the whole way, and there was a foot of snow on the ground. I almost fell over. He was talking about a *blizzard*. I laughed and laughed. It is one of my favorite memories of his childhood. It was not your average situation, but we made it through and learned so much from that time in our lives. And to be honest, our children are probably more compassionate because of it.

#Need to Know: Learn to Be a River.

Since you have *the* Rock in your life, you need to be a river. And what I mean by that is to be flexible and pliable. There is a great book by Dr. Spencer Johnson titled *Who Moved My Cheese?* It is a fantastic book about change and being flexible when you have change thrust upon you that every teen mom should read. Change is going to happen. You need to be ready for it. You need to be able to strap on your shoes and go looking for where the cheese has been moved. Life is unpredictable—just go with it! This will be a principle that you will always need to have in your life and will be applicable at all stages.

If you can't go to school right now, get a job. If you can't get a job, be well-read. A library is free; use it. Be resourceful. As a young mother who had just had her husband walk out on her, I went looking for a job that let me keep my child with me. Mainly, you'll find that in childcare, but it is a possibility. There is nothing stopping you from being witty and intelligent and making smart moves from here on out. There will be some that will place bets against you, but that's OK: let the haters hate. You keep pushing forward. I honestly do not mean this in an ugly or boastful way, and when I say keep pushing forward, I mean to do so with a humble heart. When you get where you are going in life and find success, whatever that looks like in your life, reach back and grab the hand of the girl who is struggling through what you once faced. Don't forget her. Until then, keep pushing forward.

#Need to Know: Get a Plan and Follow Through.

Just because you are very young and have found yourself in the position of being a teen mother does not mean that your life is forever altered to the point where you will not gain background that you may have lost. However, you will need to have a plan.

That's right. Sit down with someone that you see as successful and ask, "How do I get where you are? Will you be my mentor?" Write it down. Get a commitment from them and make one yourself. Making a plan that covers one year, five years, and ten years should be a great start, but honestly, in the life of a teen mother, it can start off being a three-month, six-month, and twelve-month plan. This person will be an asset to you. If you cannot find someone at the moment, start praying for one.

This is a hard step to get through and actually stay on course. I know because not only was I a teen mom, I was an outgoing, flighty, sanguine personality type. Which means I was great at being the life of the party, but follow-through was a trait that I had to acquire.

I dropped out of school in eighth grade. I have never attended a day of high school in my life, and I am now toying with the idea of getting a PhD just because I can. I love to learn and I have my MEd, so why not? What is it that you want to do, and how hard are you willing to work to get it?

#Need to Know: Choose Dignity

Maybe I am getting old, or maybe I was always born an old soul, but I believe that no matter who you are or where you are from, you decide what and who you are or will become. You can be anything, regardless of your circumstance. You do not have to be born with a silver spoon in your mouth. You do not have to be born to privilege. You do not have to be given the right opportunities to choose dignity. Anyone can have poise.

There will be people that argue, gossip, cheat, chase the next high, sleep with the best-looking guy or girl, make the most money, or live the wildest life. At this point in society, there are people that wear vice like it is a badge of honor. They live as if reality television is reality. It is not. Do not get on that level. You no longer have the luxury of living a selfish life. Be real. Be honest. Be present in your life. Your child will need you to be.

No matter what anyone tells you, there is something beautiful that comes out of struggle. I know when I write that sentence that it is a hard pill to swallow. The world wants to act like the struggle isn't there or that no one should ever have to struggle. As if somehow, we should all be born with a silver spoon in our mouths. And although no one seems to be able to clearly expound upon where this utopia is going to come from, I want to reiterate that there is something beautiful that comes from struggle.

Anyone that has spent five minutes in the life of a teen mother or single mother will tell you it is hard. But it is going to happen, so we might as well put our shoulders back and embrace it because there are two ways to handle whatever the future holds. The first is with dignity and the second is without it. Choose the former and your life will be richer for it.

#Need to Know: You Have Benefits Coming.

I am not sure you are aware of this yet, but you have benefits coming. Benefits you cannot even begin to imagine, such as seeing your great- or great-great-grand-children and being young enough to enjoy it. I have a friend whose mother had her when she was fifteen and her grandmother had her mother when she was twenty. As we met up for dinner, I realized in conversation that her grandmother is younger than my mother. My friend is blessed in so many ways by her grandmother. While both my grandmothers died years ago because of the age in which they and my mother had their children, hers is still a source of joy! I wish I had more time with both of my grandmothers. #Benefits.

When I look back over my life, I am not sure that I would have chosen to be a mom at sixteen, but I do know that given the choice now, today, I wouldn't change it for all the cherries in China. As I am writing this, I am forty-two with a twenty-six-year-old! It's wonderful having adult conversations with my daughter. We can and do laugh like crazy. During her teen years, we did not struggle with the generational gap because there wasn't one. I was that smiling face in the darkness, asking, "Where are we going? What are we doing?" When many of my daughters' peers were fighting with their parents, we didn't struggle in that area. She tells me things like, "You are going to enjoy the nursing home." I tell her that she is going to be there with me! When I am eighty-six, she will be seventy! We realize that, Lord willing, we will have each other our entire lives! It is a gift!

The truth is that more often than not, the struggle is real in the life of a teen mother or a single mother. It is also the truth that in today's society, it is practically a crime to acknowledge or (gasp!) embrace the hard things. Life has been glossed over so much that it has been narrowed down to smiling faces, always happy and successful in a Facebook post or on Instagram. It is taboo to talk about the family brawl that went down soon after the picture was taken. It is easier not to talk about the hard things. It gives everyone a false sense of security and being in control.

#Need to Know: Real Man Talk

We both know you did not get here by yourself. There is someone out there feeling just like you are. He may have totally gone AWOL or left you when you told him. He may have said hurtful things, tried to get you to abort the baby, offered to pay for the abortion, walked away, or he may have given you the silent treatment. There is no excuse for any of that. Regardless of where he is now or what he is in the future, you have to chart the course and stay on it. If he really is a great guy, great! I pray nothing but beautiful things for you with him. However, if he is not, chart a course in the opposite direction and go in that direction as fast as you can.

The "Need to Know" List

- **Put God first.**
- **Get a support system in place.**
- **Get a plan and follow through.**
- **Learn to be a river.**
- **Choose dignity.**
- **You have benefits coming.**
- **Talk about real men.**

CHAPTER 8

The Single Mother's Survival Guide

Dear Single Mama,

Take a deep breath. If you are hiding somewhere in a bathroom with the door locked, trying to find some peace while a little person's fingers are crammed under the door like a stalker's as that tiny human repeats the word, "Mommy" like it's some kind of mantra specifically made to cause that one nerve you have left to have some kind of untimely accident, I feel ya! You are not alone. My kids are almost grown and I still do this. Regardless of the circumstances that helped you arrive at this place—as in, you are the only one raising your child(ren), while the person that helped you create the angel(s) that, in all honesty, could take over the house if they joined forces, is AWOL. I need you to know that you are going to make it. There is an old saying that goes something like this: a lady is like a bag of tea—you don't really know how strong she is until you put her in hot water! And it is *true!* You are stronger than you know. You have everything you need to succeed inside you. The key is for you to figure out how to unpack the talents you have for the situation you find yourself in. But know this: greatness is already inside you.

Everything that applies to a young mom applies to you, so your list will be a little shorter here, but this is an in-addition-to list. In reality, your list is longer. Sorry! Keep reading. You are going to be just fine.

#Need to Know: This Is Only a Season.

I know that life can be overwhelming. I know that you are wearing a lot of hats and that life can seem really unfair from where you are standing. Just like in anyone else's life, there will be good days, bad days, and great days. But one day, what you have made of your todays will be memories. My daughter and I were alone for about four years, from the time she was five until she was about nine. There was a Will Smith song that was out called "Just the Two of Us." We made it our song! And before we knew it, the days turned into weeks, the weeks became months, and the years went by.

I would not have chosen single motherhood, but looking back, no matter the pain, I would not change it. It made us who we are and we are OK with that. You need to get it in your heart that regardless of your circumstances, you can make this time beautiful. You need to look into the future and see yourself looking back at the moment you are in now. There is no do-over. You get one shot.

I remember desperately wanting to go back to school, and I tried a couple of times, but it just didn't happen. I was stretched too thin and I ended up dropping out. My daughter needed my full attention, so I had a talk with God and I waited. When the time finally came, I had someone call my house and offer to help pay for it. God's timing is perfect and He opened those doors that no one else can. I have lived that out.

#Need to Know: Don't Date.

I know this seems crazy but stick with me for just a sec. I have seen more heartache and more damage done to children, relationships, and friendships by this one thing more than anything else as a single mother. I am not saying don't find someone to spend the rest of your life with. I am saying that *when or if* you decide that is the next step for your life, court instead of date. By this, I mean date with purpose. The goal is finding your forever. Not casually, and certainly not for sex.

I have some good news and some bad news. Take a deep breath for what I am about to tell you. Ready? There is no flawless knight in shining armor on a white horse coming for you. Besides, what would you do with the horse and armor afterwards? Stop having unrealistic expectations for a man. The only savior you need is Jesus. Now that we worked through that, here's the good news for you. There is a man out there that is perfect for you. One that has the strengths you need and whose hand will fit yours perfectly. The question really is, are you ready for that man?

You should look at the person you are interested in and find qualities that make that person marriage material. See how they treat others when things don't go their way. See how they treat children, especially *your* child or children because that is a deal-breaker if it's not the right fit. You do not have the luxury of messing this thing up. There is only one way for you and your children, and that is forward.

When I was single, I observed so many people making mistakes that they could not undo. They regretted those mistakes, and I wanted to learn from their mistakes, so I started praying about my husband. I didn't want to have my heart broken and I told God that. I also did not want to break anyone's heart and I told God that as well. I just wanted him to bring my husband if "my husband" was out there somewhere. He heard me. I have never dated anyone except the fathers of my children.

My husband is not perfect by any stretch of the imagination. But the things that set him apart from others for me? He was humble. He was the first one to say he was sorry. He may have had an attitude over something that bothered him, but he was also great at making course corrections and saying a simple "I'm sorry," which was so important to me. I wanted my kids to have that trait. He took my daughter as his own immediately. And I watched him walk with the

Lord. And when he needed to change something about himself, he allowed God to change him. It was incredible to watch. It still impresses me to this day.

It is possible. It doesn't matter how old-fashioned it seems or outdated. My heart and my daughter's heart were protected from men coming in and out of her life. She prayed for a father and a little brother every night, and God heard the prayers of a little eight-year-old that believed anything was possible. Somewhere in there, I got content to just live. I wasn't looking for a husband. I was the singles leader at my church at the time, and just when I settled down into my routine, God, with His funny sense of humor, shouted, "Surprise!" and in walked my husband on a Sunday morning. Kapow! Bing! Bang! Boom Shakalaka! God will work with what you give Him! Are your priorities right? Know who you are and don't compromise.

The "Need to Know" List for Single Mothers

- **Put God first.**
- **Get a support system in place.**
- **Get a plan and follow through.**
- **Learn to be a river.**
- **Choose dignity.**
- **This is only a season.**
- **Choose to court.**

CHAPTER 9

A Blended Family Road Map

I was not raised in a blended family. There were four of us kids and we all had the same mom and dad. I still remember the day in elementary school when a little girl told me her daddy didn't live with her and that her mom and dad were "divorced." I went home crying.

My husband, however, did not have the same family circumstances growing up. Two of his older sisters have their father, one older sister has her father, my husband has his father, and he has a younger brother that has a different father as well. All the siblings have a different dad except for the first two! Needless to say, they were a little blended. It's a little complicated but it is also one of the greatest gifts I have ever been given.

My daughter was nine years old when my husband and I got married. I was twenty-five and my husband was twenty-two. That means that my husband was only thirteen years older than my daughter! How we made it is a miracle! However, my mother-in-law, bless her heart, had done something years before I showed up that was absolutely the best gift she ever gave me. She raised all those children to know that family is not divided by blood. Even though her kids had different fathers, they were brothers and sisters. End of story.

When I married into that family, I didn't realize that not everyone views stepchildren as "the real deal." I learned a whole new lesson on the term "red-headed stepchild" when I talked with other blended families.

If I could take you back to Christmas or Easter around our homes to just observe, you would not be able to tell who "blood" was and who was not. My mother-in-law treated her grandchildren just like her children. She was so good to my daughter when she didn't have to be. When she succumbed to cancer twelve years after my husband and I married, someone took pictures of our kids by her bedside. My daughter lost her Nanny just like Jess did because there was never a question about who family was. I will forever be in my mother-in-law's debt for this kindness. And that, ladies and gentlemen, is how you treat the "red-headed stepchild."

#Need to Know: Figure out What Works for You and Run with It.

My mom, had she been born anywhere other than West Virginia, would have been a hippie. She was born with a wild streak and was free-spirited. She was really great at being original and she let that happen in us kids. We all have a "like us or leave us" mentality. At this point, you have read my story. You know I don't do anything in order or on someone else's timeline, so you can imagine the drama when I married a man who was a little bit of a military brat. The first time I was distracted on my way home and stopped to pick up a few things and lost my keys and spent hours looking for them in the store and didn't have a cell phone, I didn't call my husband. He was sick with worry and I was like, "What's the big deal?" It was World War III.

The first time he told me to put my seat belt on: World War III.

The first time I went over the grocery budget…you guessed it: WWIII.

There was a time I just got tired of all the expectations on me and I finally told him something I want to tell you.

This is your walk, through life. No one else can or will do it for you! Figure out what works for you as a couple and run with it. No one is going to be in your home training your children. No one is going to help you work through sticky or ugly situations. No one else is going to make peace in your home after a disagreement. No one else is living your life for you, so do not let their expectations put you in a cage that you are miserable in.

If you are good at the bills, do them. If your husband is good at the laundry, let him do it. If you are better at home repairs, do them. If he is good at getting the kids ready for bed or up in the mornings, he should do it.

Start making whatever are your strengths as strong as they can be. Then do the same for your husband or wife instead of trying to make you each strong in a role neither of you were made for. Do this despite what the world says is a "man's job" or a "woman's job."

Some of the happiest couples I know are the ones that have embraced this principle in life. They have stopped trying to make each other fit into society's mold that they will never fit in anyway and just run with what works for them.

#Need to Know: Embrace Mistakes and Learn from Them.

A mistake is a beautiful thing. I know what you're thinking—*it sure doesn't feel like a beautiful thing.* At the time, it doesn't but the truth is that a mistake, if you learn the lesson, can have significant value should you choose to allow it. My husband and I have made tons of mistakes with our kids, but inside of every mistake is the opportunity to grow in wisdom and understanding. I have watched my husband make mistakes with my daughter but then go back to her and apologize and make it right.

The lesson you need to learn may be vital to the health of your family. It may be about yourself, your spouse, your kids, or the ability to be cohesive as a family unit. But I can promise that mistakes are steps in life if you allow them to be. They are strength-building moments. As a young mother, I made so many mistakes with my daughter. I would take my frustrations out on her or not listen—really listen—to her when she was talking. I needed to pay attention and be more present in the moment, but on those days, God would use that girl to show me grace. It's OK if you aren't perfect; just commit to being a lifelong learner concerning mistakes.

#Need to Know: Never Underestimate God's Master Plan.

My husband and my ex-husband have a few things in common. First, they both stuttered as children. I asked my husband once why he didn't stutter anymore. He told me, "They told me to slow down, so I did." Second, they both have a sister named Sherrie. They both have significantly younger, blond-haired brothers whose names start with the letter "J." They both came from a blended family. They both were in my daughter's life in a profound way. It was almost as if God had an alternate plan for me, and it wasn't "Plan B."

My husband and I had a lot of opposition to our marriage. There were so many people in our lives that had opinions about us and our plans. We decided one day to exclude everyone and figure out what we wanted, as in the movie *The Notebook*, when Noah asks Allie over and over, "What do *you* want?" In the end, we eloped. When we came back from our honeymoon, the reactions were the same. People were placing bets on how long we would last.

For a while, everyone's opinions got to me and I asked God, "Were we wrong? Did we make the wrong choice? Did I not hear from you about him being my husband?" I prayed about my husband. I did. I could give you story after story where God would show me that my husband was the one and I still let the opinions of others slowly creep into my mind. I will give you one example. One particular day, I was so downhearted. I had heard something someone was saying about us and it made me so sad. I was cleaning that day and I came across a Bible I had put away and forgotten about. It was a Bible my husband gave me while we were dating. My husband had engraved my name on it with one minor adjustment. He has put his last name on it, not mine. When I opened the front page, he had inscribed it. I sat there with my hand on my chest and my mouth hanging open. He had engraved that Bible with what would be my married name, and the date he gave to me was exactly one year to the day before we randomly eloped. We were married on November 15, 2001. It was inscribed November 15, 2000, with *his* last name on the cover alongside my first name.

I honestly believe had my husband written May 14, 2000, we would have eloped on May 14 the next year. It was like God tapped me on my shoulder and said with a smile, "I knew before you did." He may not communicate with you that way, but with me, it's with a smile and an, *I told you so.* I read of a woman that refers to this kind of thing as a God wink. He was totally winking at me that day, and I needed it!

You see, regardless of how you view yourself, regardless of how other people may see you, the only thing that really matters is how God sees you. It took a lot of heartache and hurt for me to realize this. It is true because you see, one day, when we stand before God, He will say, "Well done, [my] good and faithful servant." His opinion is the only one that matters, and He has a plan that was set into motion long before you were even a thought in your parents' minds, your great-grandparents' minds, and even your ancestors' minds a thousand years ago.

I can see Him now. He starts planning me. He leans back in his chair (not your average chair, like a chair made from gold that glows from the light of stars). He cocks his head to one side and then the other side, shrugs His shoulder and says to Himself, "Why not?" So, He leans forward and gets to work. He throws in a dash of crazy, a big heart, a little mischievousness (not too much, who knows what she could get into), a bushel of loyalty, a little temper here and there, a little moxie, and a bit of artsy-get-losty. Ladies and gentlemen, when He is finished with the thought that will be me, He leans back with tears rolling down His face and roars with laughter. "This is gonna be great!" He knows who I am down to the number of hairs on my head. Truth be told, I always wanted to be tall, thin, statuesque, and graceful, commanding a room when I walk in. God thought the better version of me would be a little shorter, fatter, and funnier…just like my mama.

His plan is so much bigger than what you can know or comprehend. It is the same with you, your children, and your family, however that family may look. He sees them the same way He sees you from a long time ago, and with great thought and care.

#Need to Know: Give Everyone Time to Fall in Love!

My final thought for all of the blended families in the world? Jesus came from one. He must have seen the value of such a thing if it is done well. I tell my husband all the time that he is doing the same things Joseph did, so he must be special. Joseph in the Bible was a lot like my dad. He was not flashy or in your face. He was strong with good character. He was steady. He was exactly what was needed for Jesus, the greatest story ever told.

If you have remarried and have a decent man that is the stepfather to your children, honor him. Respect him. Encourage him. Believe in him. Give him time to love your kids by not making him the disciplinarian right off the bat. Help your kids learn to trust and love him so when he corrects them, they feel loved despite the correction, as they do when you correct them! Pray over their relationship. This applies to stepmothers as well. The principle is the same. Let the birth parent do the correcting in the beginning for a little while, become a united front, and slowly, children will feel safe and loved by this new parent in their life. You should always keep in mind that they did not ask for the changes in the relationship that have been thrust upon them. They can be victims or beneficiaries in the transition and formation of a new family; you decide what they are.

And then one day, when you least expect it, your child will need a parent and they reach for your spouse's hand and not yours. And you will know that you've done it right. You built the bridge. Bravo on a job well done!

The "Need to Know" List for Blended Families

- **Put God first.**
- **Figure out what works for you and run with it.**
- **Embrace mistakes and learn from them.**
- **Never underestimate God's master plan.**
- **Give everyone time to fall in love.**

CHAPTER 10

Finding "The" Guy

Girls, we cannot have a book about unplanned pregnancy without having a talk about the boys. They are the other half of the equation here. They are the reason for the butterflies. They are the reason your breath gets taken away. They are the reason we throw all caution to the wind. They hold out their beautiful hands and say *come with me*. We take one look into their eyes and off we go. I have a confession. This happened to me. It's true. The day I laid eyes on my husband, I was lost. I mean, gone. Put a fork in me. I was done. The good news is that, even though we had a ton of issues and dysfunction, he had great character. The best parts of him were the parts that I needed. We just celebrated our eighteenth anniversary. True story.

My sister called me one time laughing over an article she read that said the chemicals in our brains that are present during the falling in love stage are the same ones found in people who are crazy. Like psych-ward cray. Those feelings have to subside at some point or we would all go insane. Honestly, just writing it still makes me laugh. This is one of the best parts…falling in love. Finding *that* guy.

So, we need to talk about it for a second. As I write this book, I currently work at a pregnancy center. We see all manner of girls; they come in all shapes and sizes, and we see all creeds, colors, and cultures. Girls wearing hijabs. Girls with crosses around their necks. Girls with no beliefs. Girls that are confused. Girls that are happy and girls that are heartbroken.

We also have guys come in on a regular basis; they sit quietly in the waiting room trying to be as inconspicuous as possible, almost like if they move too quickly, they will upset the estrogen balance in the building. They are uneasy and outnumbered and they know it. Many times, they are young, and we really do make an effort to make them feel at ease and know that we value them as well as the client walking in the door. We do this because we know what society has done. We know that most of the time, they do not feel they should have a voice and so they force her to make any and all decisions. Sometimes, they pressure her to get rid of it. They offer to pay for it. They bargain. They get angry. They think of how it will affect their own lives, and the most convenient thing to do is to leave it to the women to make the decision. To carry the guilt or the baby alone.

However, we also see the extraordinary guy come through our doors. He looks like all the others. You couldn't pick him out from the others except that fatherhood changes him. His response to this cataclysmic change is evident. My best friend called me when her grandson was born. I asked how her son was taking it and she said he can't stop crying. If you knew Larry, you would know that this was completely out of character for him. He is not a soft, touchy-feely kind of guy. He drives a jeep and has two boys. He can be mouthy and sarcasm is like one of his love languages, but he had the good stuff in him. The moment his son came into this world, he was changed forever.

Girls, no matter what package he comes in, look for *that* guy. If you got pregnant by one of those guys, you will know immediately. They come in with you to the doctor's appointment. They make sure you are OK. Fatherhood for them started the moment you told them, not the moment you gave birth. I am not saying to expect perfection because that is unrealistic and it will set you and your relationship up for failure. You're not perfect. (Gasp!) So please allow for some imperfection. Be kind. Learn to compromise on the little things so you never have to compromise on the big things.

At the center, I see both kinds of men—the forever changed and unfortunately, the unchanged. They walk in. Big. Small. Short. Tall. Unsure. Confident. Tattooed. Tattoo-less. They get called back for the ultrasound and they are changed. They grab her hand or lean back against the wall to brace themselves. They say something or maybe nothing at all. But you could see it. I always love to go in with couples because while she watches the screen, he watches her and the screen, and I watch him. It's like those videos on YouTube that make you cry when they show the groom's reaction to the bride coming down the aisle. It is exactly like that. A defining moment. A rip in the timeline of his life. I have left tough men sitting in a chair only to come back and find that tough guy with red eyes and a red face, barely holding it together. When I am given the opportunity to be there, I often tell them what I see by looking them in the face and telling them, "You are going to be a great father; I just know it."

I have walked back into my office after appointments like these and cried. I have thanked God for the man that he may not even know that he is. I thanked God that *his heart* was touched by that little heart beating on the screen. I have sat at my desk and prayed for other men that miss this. I pray that there are more men like ones that are changed. I have prayed for every guy that wasn't overjoyed at the heartbeat. The guy for whom fear is greater than anything at that moment. I pray that fear would go so hope and love and faith could grow.

When you decide you are looking for a guy, there are tons of small particulars that do not matter. Style doesn't matter. Honestly, money doesn't matter. Color doesn't matter. But these things matter: having some grit, standing up for what you believe in, honesty, loyalty, and strong moral character when no one is looking—those are a few non-negotiables. My husband, even at a young age, was full of grit. He met me when he was nineteen. I was twenty-one and I had a six-year-old daughter. That means, ladies and gentlemen, that when my daughter was born, my husband was thirteen. (Take a deep breath; we hadn't met yet!) When we were first married, he went to pick her up at school and they told her that her brother was there to get her. They had different last names. He had a babyface, and the math was just too impossible. She was so confused until she got to the office and saw who it was picking her up. She exclaimed, "That's not my brother! That's my dad!"

How we made it this far is only because of grace and our willingness to overcome the impossible. Look for *that* guy. One that will face the odds that are against you and find a way to make it work. Look for the humble. Look for the smart. Look for servants—men unafraid to serve others. Look for men that serve God and strive to be like Christ. Trust your instincts. Find the man that is more concerned about *you* than himself. And then, the standard that you hold them to, make that your standard as well. If you expect kindness, be kind. If you expect a man to treat you with love and respect, be prepared to treat him that way. If you expect greatness, then rise up to be the girl that is deserving of that greatness.

If you are a hot mess and you know it, take a moment off from trying to find the one and work on yourself. Work through your issues and make yourself well because if you do find Mr. Right and you are not prepared, you can miss that opportunity. You can do more harm than good, and that is not the goal.

If you have no idea what healthy relationships look like, start reading. Find resources. Find a couple that you really admire and ask them to mentor you and your partner. There are ways to stop the cycle of being unable to change. It *can* begin with you.

CHAPTER 11

Unplanned Pregnancies of Biblical Proportions

Throughout the Bible, there are instances of unplanned pregnancies that changed the world. Our very Christian faith starts and hinges on an unplanned pregnancy, so I will start there. I am sharing these with you to simply point out that while some people may look down on you, you can take comfort in knowing they would probably be the same people to look down on Mary. *The mother of God.* Insert eye roll and big grin here.

I want to point out a couple of things to you. First, you are not the first or last girl with things not going the way you planned. At this point in my life, I am going to start calling the plans I make the un-plans because if I know anything, I know that today I may be in a dungeon but tomorrow I could wake up in a palace. I could tell plenty of biblical stories where this literally happened to men. Hello, Joseph! But for now, we are going to stick with the girls of the Bible with the unplanned and impossible situations they found themselves in. Sister—if you think you have it rough, take the worst day you have ever had and subtract indoor plumbing and electricity. Oh— no pain meds for delivery and absolutely no hospital for your baby to be in. Cue the tent. Their culture was less forgiving, their situations hopeless, and they persevered. They weren't magical beings, but flesh and blood just like you and me. If they can put on their big girl panties and deal with life, so can we. You are not alone!

Mary and Elizabeth

In biblical times, a woman's most valued roles were as an unmarried virgin in her father's house or as a child-bearing woman in her husband's house. You can see this in stories throughout the Bible, with the exception of the first chapter of Luke. You see that this story begins with not one unplanned pregnancy, but two. One would bring shame to the woman, and the other would bring redemption.

The first chapter of Luke tells of the conception of Christ. In this passage, there are two women involved. One woman was a virgin that was about to be disgraced by an unprecedented and very unplanned pregnancy. The other is a barren woman that had already been disgraced by the inability to give her husband children.

People often act as if Mary were as calm as God himself in her demeanor, but in Luke 1:29, she was troubled just from the greeting of the angel, and all he had done was compliment her since his arrival. She was unable to see in herself what God saw in her, which is often the case in ourselves. When I read it, I could hear her asking, "What is *that* supposed to mean?"

So, the angel tells her, "You have found favor with God. You are going to have a baby and not just any baby."

So, Mary responds, "Am I now? That's impossible. Really, really impossible." (I am paraphrasing.)

The angel proceeds to tell her what her future holds and as a confirmation, he tosses her barren cousin Elizabeth into the deal so she doesn't have to go through it alone. Then he wraps it all with a nice bow by saying, "Nothing is impossible with God."

She knows this is true; her only answer is agreement. "So be it."

Sure enough, Mary visits her cousin, and she is expecting as well. Elizabeth and her husband were too old to have a baby, and when Zachariah pointed this out to the angel, his lack of faith cost him his voice until after his baby was born. As soon as Mary arrived at her cousin's house, Elizabeth's unborn baby recognized the baby Mary was carrying and leaped in her womb. Elizabeth immediately proclaimed that Mary was blessed among women. The baby that Elizabeth carried would be born and named John. John would prepare the way of Christ. He would baptize Jesus Christ himself in the Jordan River.

Thousands of years later, through every land, language, and people group, the Christmas celebration has grown and changed. New traditions have come and given families a sense of who they are in the world. Lights are strung, trees decorated and put up, cookies are baked, gifts are given; across the world, music is played glorifying God in the highest. Peace on earth is prayed for and proclaimed. At my house, we all gather round after the food and before the gifts and we read the story of Jesus' birth. We laugh and sometimes we cry. We give thanks to a Savior who, while we were yet sinners, while we were yet to be born, saw our value and was born just so *He* could die an excruciating death as payment for our sin. And it all started with a couple of unplanned pregnancies.

Sarah

Sarah is the wife of Abraham in the Bible. This woman's unplanned pregnancy, as well as the lack of pregnancy and her efforts to resolve the problem, have shaped the world in its impact. There is not a mother in the Bible whose unplanned pregnancy impacted more people other than Mary. Sarah is regarded as a matriarch of the three major monotheistic faiths: Christianity, Judaism, and Islam.

Sarah and Abraham are promised a son by God. Time comes and goes with no sign of a baby in sight. They grow older and older without the promise showing up until finally, Sarah takes things into her own hands. She tells Abraham to marry her servant, Hagar, and make a baby so that she may have a child through her. Hagar becomes pregnant and Sarah can't stand it. She sends Hagar away, where an angel finds her and tells her everything will be OK. He tells her to go back home and have her baby and call him Ishmael, which she does. This baby grows up to be a pretty important guy. He is considered by Muslims to be the father of the Arab people. Well, that was unplanned.

This still doesn't solve the problem of Sarah not having the baby God promised to her and Abraham. She laughed when she was told she would get pregnant despite her age. When she finally gets pregnant, she is ninety years old. Isaac arrives on the scene and grows to become the father of Jacob and Esau, another set of VIPs from the Bible. Abraham is considered a patriarch of the Jewish and Christian faiths. I can assure you that Sarah wasn't planning on any of this story unfolding the way that it did, as evidenced in the laughter when told she would have a baby at ninety.

CHAPTER 12

Resources: (What Now? What's Next?)

When it comes to guiding someone to resources, I needed to make them broad enough that the list could be used universally. The list needed to help someone in Tennessee as well as someone in Utah. It obviously cannot be a detailed list for every community across the nation. The list I have compiled for you is full of resources available in almost every community, but they may look different in your community. Meaning that you may have to look a little harder than someone else, or you may find exactly what you are looking for on your first try.

The truth is that it is more important to present you with principles to guide you through rough terrain more than a list that you check off as you go. Because what happens when you operate with a set of rules and you encounter something that the rules don't cover? You are unsure of what to do. My goal is to get you thinking and developing your problem-solving skills for your situation rather than going by what I tell you to do.

Learn to Be Resourceful

Resourceful: having the ability to find quick and clever ways to overcome difficulties.

The great news about this principle is that being resourceful now is a lot easier than it used to be. Now there are enough online resources about every subject under the planet that you literally can find just about any answer you need. Then there is that moment where the rubber meets the road. You look up how to manage your money and there are awesome tips, but you look down and there isn't enough money to pay the bills. Being resourceful is figuring out the space between whatever options you have before you and making it work for you.

Moving to a new neighborhood

When I was younger, I was divorced and my daughter and I were living with my sister and her son. Neither of us made a lot of money and we were living in a rough part of town. We decided that it was not a good place for our kids, but weren't sure how to go about changing it. Finally, one day I loaded everyone in the car, made a leap of faith, and took off driving out to the country, telling everyone we were going to find a house. We drove up and down country back roads, until we came across a house. A little brick rancher that was empty. There were no signs around except a no trespassing sign hanging on the road beside it. We knocked on a neighbor's house and found out about the owners who lived next door. He told us to disregard the no trespassing sign and to go down that road to talk with the owners. We did and the owner drove us back up to the house and let us look through it. He was interested in renting it but just hadn't put it on the market yet. He let us rent that house, and soon enough, we moved in. We stayed in that house for years. Our kids went to a great school. We built some really great memories there that would never have been made without a leap of faith and some resourcefulness.

Show me the money

When my daughter's father left us, I had a hard time paying for childcare, so I looked for a job that allowed me to take my daughter to work with me. I was a nanny for several years until my daughter started school. I actually made some decent money during that time and I had no childcare bill to pay. Oh, that every single mom or young mom could find such a situation. You are able to get more done than you know! Look for a way to fill the space between your options and your reality. You can do this!

> "If you want something, you must become relentless for success, resourceful for what you need, and resistant to excuses."
> —Anonymous

Learn to be Creative

Creative: relating to or involving the imagination or original ideas, especially in the production of artistic work.

I'm not going to lie. I may be a little jealous. You have Pinterest as a resource. I lose hours of my life on that website and walk away thinking I don't have a creative bone in my body. Your life as a mom, especially as a mom on a limited income, is going to require a little creativity. Honestly, just give yourself the title of creative director and get it over with.

"Creativity is just connecting things. When you ask creative people how they did something, they feel a little guilty because they didn't really do it, they just saw something. It seemed obvious to them after a while. That's because they were able to connect experiences they've had and synthesize new things."
—Steve Jobs

When my daughter was young, we did not have a lot of money, but we sure had time and our imagination. When her birthdays rolled around, a sleepover was usually the order of the day. We had baby pools in the front yard and spoon races. We sang songs and watched movies. Some of my favorite memories are of her and her friends gathered around, playing in the yard in bathing suits. They didn't have a clue it was because I really could not afford that overpriced, unappetizing pizza served at that place with the big mouse (not naming names here) that is just a casino for kids, anyway. Talk about a money pit.

Being creative will help you in every area of your life: daily living, special occasions, finances, school projects, and just about every other area. A woman who is resourceful *and* creative is a force to be reckoned with.

Learn to Be a Problem-Solver

Problem-solving: the process of working through details of a problem to reach a solution.

Honestly, this is one of my biggest pet peeves. Or rather it's linked to one, which is complaining. People who complain are usually not problem-solvers. They like cheese to go with that whine. It drives me crazy. There is a scene in the movie *A Bug's Life*. All the ants are marching in a line when a leaf falls from a tree. The ant at the front of the line freezes and starts screaming that he's lost and yelling for help! In rushes another ant calling himself a professional; he helps the ant walk *around* the leaf. The scene is humorous, but truth be

> *"Don't bother people for help without first trying to solve the problem yourself."*
> —Colin Powell

told, we all know someone who is like that first ant. They have a wrench thrown into their plan and suddenly they are paralyzed with indecision. They don't know what the next move should be so they get stuck. Do *not* be that ant. Be bold and decisive. There is a hilarious meme that floats around Facebook every few years that states, "Be decisive...right or wrong...the road of life is paved with flat squirrels who couldn't make a decision." Life is going to give you plenty of obstacles. Find a solution. Make a decision. Walk around the leaf.

Be Well-Read

Well-read: knowledgeable and informed as a result of extensive reading.

Being well educated can cost thousands of dollars and the roll of the dice to get a good professor or teacher. But being well-read is an entirely different matter. You do not need a PhD to be well-read. You can, however, stand in a room with people that have their PhDs and carry on a conversation intelligently by being well-read. There are no restrictions. Pick a topic that interests you and dive into it! By the time you do arrive ready to earn a degree, you can be well-versed in the topic of your choice, which can only improve your grades.

I have met people that were knowledgeable about a topic that were by no means experts in that field, but they were passionate and well-read, and to me, just as fascinating to listen to as an expert would be. It is a gift to be able to carry on a conversation with people that have a different skill set than

"The more that you read, the more things you will know. The more that you learn, the more places you'll go."
—Dr. Seuss

you, maybe more education, as well as people of various backgrounds and leave them impressed!

It can open doors for you and all it takes is a moment stolen here and there to read. The library is a great place to start. Free Wi-Fi can take you to so many reputable places: The National Archives, political commentary, local resources, and organizations that specialize in helping those that are in your shoes! There are people in history who worked very hard to make sure that free education was a right for everyone. Take advantage of the gift of knowledge you can use! I hope you get off social media and get to building your knowledge of the world. You are able, you have a mind, you have eyes. Use them to create something great.

Final and Practical Resources

» Health department: If this is an issue and you don't know where else to go, many health departments help with everything from ob-gyn exams to sexually transmitted disease testing.

» Nonprofit organizations: Organizations such as Heartbeat International and Care Net can help you get a free pregnancy test and ultrasound or maybe your first supply of prenatal vitamins at no charge.

» Young Life: This organization is set up to help teen moms have a community with others navigating being a young mom! They help set you up for success.

» Local Mom groups: Find a Mothers of Preschoolers (MOPS) group that you can connect with. In my area, we have a group called Thrive for single moms to get support and fellowship that is awesome! They are out there!

» Social media: I am adding this because it *can* be a valuable resource! I do want to caution that many times what we see on social media is not real life—it is a filtered version of reality that only shows the highlights of others' lives. Everyone posts accomplishments and vacations; no one wants to talk about crying themselves to sleep the night before or living with real disappointments. Find blogs that encourage you or challenge you. Use this resource as a weapon in your hand to win a battle—the one for your mind and future!

» Library: A *free* resource in your community. Use it! You can learn how to write a résumé, get online to fill out job applications, or find an apartment. You can teach your kids how to be quiet and respectful in a public place and show them a love for reading and learning at an early age. Look for books that will build your faith and encourage you.

» Speaking of books—I have several that I think would be very helpful for the different situations discussed in this book.

» Telling your parents:

- Jayne E. Schooler, *"Mom, Dad…I'm Pregnant": When Your Daughter or Son Faces an Unplanned Pregnancy* (NavPress, 2004).

» Overwhelming emotions:

- Leslie Leyland Fields, *Surprise Child: Finding Hope in an Unexpected Pregnancy* (WaterBrook, 2006).

» Post-abortion help:

- Wendy Giancola, *Transforming Your Story: A Path to Healing After Abortion* (Merrifield Press, 2016).

- Lorraine Marie Varela, *Planned from the Start: A Healing Devotional* (Romans 8:28 Books, 2016).

» Social services: Your area more than likely has a social services department, and if they are really on top of things, you can be connected to just about every resource your community has to offer, from finding childcare to abuse shelters to homeless shelters and everything in between. Use it!

» Legal Aid: This is a charitable organization that helps people with little money receive legal help. When my daughter's father left, this was how I was able to get my divorce papers filed at no cost. He left and was gone for a couple of years. I was a single mom with no money and no idea how to get a divorce. I called around and found them. It was a hassle and it took a while, but all in all, it was finished and that chapter in my life was finally over, so a new one could begin.

» Safe Haven Laws: Please learn the safe haven laws in your state. A great place to start is at www.nationalsafehavenalliance.org. There are laws that were created to protect and save babies as well as their mothers from prosecution should they need to surrender their babies because they cannot take care of them. An infant never need be abandoned. There are police stations, fire stations, and hospitals that will help you, no questions asked!

As We Part Ways...

I hope you take to heart what I have written in these pages. I hope you grab the bull we call life, by the horns and wrestle it to the ground. I pray you know who you are and your value. I pray you fully realize the privilege you have been given in being called Mom…even if at times that looks *tore up from the floor up*. I hope you are equipped to create something beautiful of what you have been given and that twenty years from now, you will look back and know you pulled off the impossible with God by your side.

You may choose to write books, raise kids, travel the world, fight human trafficking, be journalists, doctors, teachers, firefighters, be scientists, or become artists. Whatever you do, know this: I may never meet you, but in my heart, I have been cheering for you as I was writing!

Your value is set and it's priceless.

You are strong.

You are a fighter, even when you don't feel like it.

ACKNOWLEDGMENTS

A dam, my love, thank you for putting up with me staring at my laptop for days. Thank you for all you do!

Miranda and Jess—you are my greatest treasures. Thank you for being my biggest cheerleaders.

Thank you to every woman sharing their story in these pages—you are beautiful.

Dayna—you are an artist, thank you!

Rebecca M. and Megan—Thank you for the photographs and the laughs.

Last but not least—Rachel Shuster. Thank you for the first edits and kindness. You are awesome.

ABOUT THE AUTHOR

Sarah Dunford, once a middle-school dropout and teen mom, is the author of *Parenthood Unplanned: A Survival Guide for the Unexpected.* She is passionate about helping others face the challenges that come with life's sometimes impossible and unexpected circumstances, having faced similar situations firsthand. From the depths of heartache and uncertainty, Sarah went on to earn her B.A. in history from Virginia Commonwealth University and her M.A. in education from Liberty University. She currently serves as the Client Services Director for her local pregnancy center.